A WORLD OF FLAVOURS

Tapas

A WORLD OF FLAVOURS

Tapas

Authentic regional recipes

M Teresa Segura

APPLE

A Quintet Book

First published in the UK in 2009 by
Apple Press
7 Greenland Street
London NW1 OND
United Kingdom

www.apple-press.com

Cover photo © Garlick, Ian / Stockfood America

ISBN: 978 1 84543 321 5
QTT.WFSP

This book was conceived, designed and produced by
Quintet Publishing Limited
6 Blundell Street
London N7 9BH
United Kingdom

Project Editor: Robert Davies
Designer: Rod Teasdale
Art Director: Michael Charles
Managing Editor: Donna Gregory
Publisher: James Tavendale
Additional Text: Camilla Barton, Diana Craig

Printed and bound in Singapore

10 9 8 7 6 5 4 3 2 1

Contents

Introduction

Spanish food is fresh, healthy, flavourful and uncomplicated and is based on the produce which is grown and sold locally. This cuisine is the perfect match for modern tastes, which lean towards simple food with bold flavours. This book introduces a range of Spanish tastes, from the classic tapas popular in bars across the country to more sophisticated dishes which show off the finest produce of the different regions. These recipes can all be used in different ways, according to what suits you – the serving information suggests which dishes are best served alone, and which can also be prepared as part of a tapas feast. What all 100 recipes have in common is their freshness, simplicity and fine flavours.

Taberna La Ardosa, Madrid.

The regions of Spain

Though its borders are clearly defined, Spain has been a single country for fewer than 500 years – so it is unsurprising that each region is more conscious of its individual identity than of its Spanish nationality. For the different regions, food has become a prominent expression of local identity. The mountain ranges which run across the peninsula have also played a large part in making the cuisine of each community distinct from that enjoyed by neighbouring regions – especially because, until the last half of the twentieth century, transportation between the regions was difficult.

There are, though, themes which run through the cooking of the whole country and which make it possible to speak of a distinctively Spanish style of cooking. The Moors, who stayed for nearly a millennium, influenced the cooking of the south of Iberia, in particular, and the ingredients they introduced remain popular.

The struggle to throw out the Moors brought a second influence to Spanish food. Because Muslims do not eat pork, this meat became a key ingredient and the cooking of pork was elevated to a position of real respect in Christian Spanish society.

A third common idea is the respect for and interest in fine ingredients. Many countries claim to produce the finest foods in Europe, but Spain is a strong contender. Its harvests of olives, citrus fruits, peppers and rice are of an extremely high standard. Wine- and sherry-making are crafts which have long been cultivated. Spanish cooks are extremely skilled at devising simple recipes designed to show off their food without unnecessary complications. The recipes in this book all derive from these centuries-old traditions. The food featured here, and the food enjoyed across Spain, may be straightforward – but it is extremely tasty.

The North (Galicia, Asturias, Cantabria)

Northern Spain has a climate and landscape far different from that of the coastal regions of the south – and this is reflected in the local food. The coast is buffeted by strong Atlantic winds and queimada is its antidote. This punch is made from Galician aguardiente – a spirit distilled from wine and flavoured with herbs or coffee, plus sugar, lemon peel, coffee beans and cinnamon. Fantastic fish stews are made here, as the north coast provides some of the best shellfish and seafood in Europe, including octopus, oysters, huge orange mussels, scallops and rock lobsters.

Galicia, the north-west corner of Spain, has a Celtic heritage, bagpipe music, a rainy climate and rugged coastlines. The region supplies the whole of Spain with cabbages, turnips and potatoes. The best-known dishes are broths with cabbage, like caldo gallego and lacon con grelos, a ham knuckle with young turnip tops. Unique to the area are empanadas – flat pies filled with shellfish, sardines or pork, and bell peppers. An almond tart is a Galician speciality made to celebrate Saint James's Day. Local recipes rarely include olive oil or garlic. In the hillier but poorer south, chestnut trees are prolific and chestnuts are eaten like potatoes are elsewhere.

To the east of Galicia lies Asturias, a region noted for its wild forests. Known for producing the best milk in Spain, Asturias is home to the famous cabrales, a blue-veined cheese aged in natural caves in the limestone mountains of the area. There are over two dozen varieties of cow's, sheep's and goat's milk cheeses.

This area is home to many varieties of apple, used to fill warm apple pies and make strong sparkling cider. Being a European wilderness, pigeon, partridge, red deer, trout and salmon are found in abundance.

A popular destination for Spanish family holidays, the Cantabrian coast to the east of Asturias boasts excellent seafood. This lush, green province is known for its fine dairy products and cheese-based desserts such as quesada pasiega. Away from the coast, the climate favours cattle-breeding and dishes focus on meat, which is grilled or stewed. Beef, ox, deer, roe deer or boar are used. Typical main meals are cocido montañés (Highlander stew) made with beans, meat, cabbage and potato and cocido lebaniego (Liébanan stew) made with meat and chick peas.

Houses by the coast in Cudillero – a fishing village in Asturias, on the ancient route of pilgrimage called the Way of Saint James.

The Pyrenees (Navarre, Basque Country, Aragon)

The Basque country in north-east Spain has a long tradition of fine cooking and its people are considered Spain's most devoted cooks, with recipes handed down through generations and gastronomic societies everywhere. Being next to both the Bay of Biscay and the mountains that lead to France, there are several different styles of cooking and the meals often reflect a French influence. Traditional Basque cuisine focuses on seafood, especially the salt cod, which is often cooked in a peppery sauce. Hake, sole, spider crab, baby eels, line-caught squid and shellfish also dominate. Some more unusual delicacies are fresh hake cheeks, wild boar, sea urchins and calves' snouts and brains. The mountains provide fine meat and game, dairy products, vegetables and wild mushrooms. Flavourful sauces are made with herbs, tomatoes and bell peppers. Chocolate is a local passion and txakoli is a light wine perfect with seafood.

Navarre, to the east, enjoys a temperate climate with mountains and green valleys in the north and dusty plains in the south. The region is the largest tomato producer in Spain and the description 'a la Navarra' means 'with tomatoes'. One classic dish from Navarre involves pan-frying mountain-stream trout stuffed with cured ham and served on a bed of tomatoes and onions. Lovely vegetables are cultivated in the warm Ebro valley and often cooked in a vegetable stew 'menestre'. Tudela is famous for its asparagus which is made into tortillas and pointed spicy red peppers are best from Lodoso. These pimientos del pico are stuffed with meat or salt cod to make a delicious meal. Wheat, corn and vineyards that bottle popular wines are also found here. High in the mountains, lambs are reared for dishes like cochifrito and chilindron, wild rabbits are stewed with snails and herbs and pigeons are added to a raisin and pine nut sauce.

Aragon is a large, wealthy region with five climate zones and contrasting landscapes. The Pyrenees tower in the north and the Ebro, the largest river in Spain, crosses Aragon from west to east. Perfect conditions in northern areas include green meadows ideal for lamb and beef breeding, and the upper river valleys provide trout, salmon, boar, truffles and mushrooms to the region. The lower irrigated areas grow expanses of wheat, barley, rye, fruit and grapes for wine. Terul's famous ham is delicious cooked with red bell peppers al chilindron. A traditional dish of salt cod flavoured with red peppers is enjoyed here, as well as other seafood combinations such as crab paste.

Benasque – a small town nestling in the heart of the Pyrenees.

The best and freshest food in Barcelona is to be found in markets like this one, where a huge array of Iberian foodstuffs are sold.

Catalonia

Catalonia in the north-east boasts the most sophisticated Spanish regional cuisine, perhaps due to the combination of mountain and coastal locales and the common border with France. The capital Barcelona has enjoyed a reputation for over 150 years as a city of good eating. Spain's alternative to champagne, called cava, is produced in Sant Sadurní d'Anoia, nearby.

Adventurous pairings like lobster and chicken, lobster and chocolate sauce and goslings with figs are common in Catalonia. Zarzuela and suquet – gorgeous fish stews – are the highlights on this region's menu. Other stews include beans with the local fat white sausage called butifarra – made of pork and spices. Various Catalan sauces enrich the meat and seafood flavours, including allioli, romesco, picada and samfaina. Bacalao con samfaina pairs salt cod with a tomato, pepper and aubergine sauce and grilled seafood is delicious with the chilli and hazelnut romesco sauce. All meals come with tomato-coated bread, pan con tomate. Creamy desserts, like curds with honey and the local crème brûlée, crema Catalana, are popular.

While there are many popular rice dishes here, pasta such as cannelloni is sometimes used. A traditional lobster dish, called rossejat de fideos, resembles paella but instead of rice, it has fideos – fine vermicelli-like pasta. Catalans celebrate both the hunting and eating of local mushrooms, particularly rovellos, during the mushroom festival in autumn. The prized pickings are shown to the townspeople, then the mushrooms are lovingly sautéed in olive oil and garlic and garnished with parsley.

The East (Murcia, Valencia, the Balearic Islands)

Murcia, a small region of south-eastern Spain, is by no means small in the way of culinary offerings. Home of several excellent wineries and delicately flavoured rice from Calasparra, the region boasts top-quality products that go into and accompany its food. Local rice dishes include arroz con conejo y caracoles – rice with rabbit and snails – and other combinations of vegetables, chicken or beans. Irrigation systems put in place by the Moors centuries ago help the region to keep producing vast quantities of fresh fruits, vegetables and flowers. Murcian specialities include the omelette-style zarangollo – tomato, courgette, onion and egg – and the small pasty pastel de carne, filled with meat, tomatoes and egg. Mar Menor, a salty lagoon on the coast of Murcia, provides wonderful fish and shellfish, used in a variety of ways. There's the fish soup sopa de pescado and salty fish such as the roe huevas, pescadoa a la sal – typically bass or grey mullet baked in salt and escabeche – fished baked in oil and vinegar.

Valencia, east of Murcia, is a sharp contrast to its neighbour. While Murcia is one of the hottest and driest territories in Europe, Valencia occupies fertile land called the huerta. Orange, lemon and peach groves abound and rice fields, also harbouring eels, cover the farmland. Rice is made into paella or cooked in a fish stock and served with allioli. Eels are popular and cooked with garlic and paprika. In the summer, the ice-cold milky drink horchata is served, made from tigernuts, water and sugar.

The Balearic Islands off the eastern coast – including Majorca, Menorca, Ibiza and Formentera – have a long history of various cultures sweeping over them, which have all contributed to the area's food. Fresh fish is often on the menu, such as rock lobster which is cooked with herb-flavoured spirits and the fish stew zarzuela. Solid peasant vegetable dishes like oliagua soups and tumbet also feature as well as the local paprika and blood sausage sobrasada. The sausage is used in sofrit pages – an island stew of gently spiced pork, lamb, chicken, peppers, potatoes and a rich aromatic sauce. Excellent pizzas called coca are made here with four main varieties: sweet, savoury, closed and open. Mayonnaise originated in Menorca, although the French left the islands after occupation in the 1770s and took it as their own. The English around this time left behind their gin, which is still widely drunk on the islands today. Ibizan desserts such as the almond cake gato d'Ametlla and the cheesecake flaò are both popular. However, the light pastry ensaimada is the island's treasure – similar to a croissant, it is filled with chocolate or cream or eaten plain with sugar.

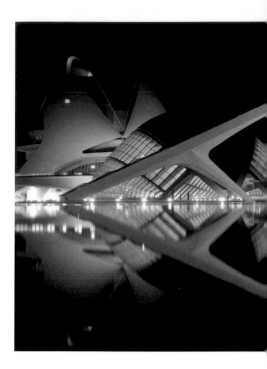

Valencia is famed for its combination of a rich architectural, culinary and cultural history with a cutting-edge approach to design, food and nightlife.

The Parque del Buen Retiro in Madrid is a popular place for the city's inhabitants to relax.

Central and Western Spain (Castile, La Mancha, Madrid, Extremadura)

Due to its central location, Madrid was given the role of Spain's capital 400 years ago. The city's inhabitants enjoy their meat, including thick steaks and milk-fed veal from Avila. Cocido madrileño, from Madrid, is one of Spain's national dishes – a vast cauldron of meats, vegetables, chick peas and herbs that simmers all day to create this meal. Tapas bars are plentiful for tourists and residents alike, with complimentary hot or cold tastings of the tuna delicacy mojama, potato omelette tortilla de patata, prawns and the Spanish ham jamón, among many others.

The interior of Spain is defined by countryside cuisine with heart-warming stews and roasts of lamb, suckling pig cochinillo and goat cooked in old Arab beehive ovens. The cold air on the high plateau during winter is perfect for curing various meats and cheeses, such as the cured sheep's cheese queso manchego. Castile and Leon (unified in 1983), north of Madrid over the Guadarrama mountains, is sometimes referred to as Spain's bread basket – fine wheat is grown here and turned into large, round, white loaves. Small areas have their own specialities, such as Sepulveda's suckling lamb, the tiny roast piglets of Arevolo and the sweet yellow cakes of Avila. The poorer families of Castile and Leon eat beans, lentils and chick peas, as in the tasty bean and sausage dish called garbanzos con chorizos.

South of Madrid is Castile La Mancha, known for sunflowers, olive groves, windmills and Don Quixote. Manchego cheese originates here, as well as the tortilla. The hard climate of bitterly cold winters and harsh summers has bred strong, raw tastes. Common foods include garlic soups, meatballs, chick peas and dishes flavoured with thyme and cumin. These flavourings arrived with the Arabs who also planted saffron, which is now thought to be the finest in the world. Pisto manchego is a blend of tomatoes and vegetables that is served either hot or cold, as a main dish or starter. Partridges are used to make pâté, or cooked with wine and vinegar.

Andalusia

Andalusia is the epitome of all things the tourist thinks of as typically Spanish – sangria, bullfighting, flamenco dancing, olive groves and orange trees. It covers one-sixth of the country and has five coastal provinces, with sunny tourist beaches along the coast. In contrast, the high mountains of Grenada have cold winters and host skiing until May. Seafood is prevalent in Andalusia, with fried fish pescaito frito from Cadiz a speciality. Along the Costa del Sol are sold battered squid rings, calamares, as are fish soups, stews of shark, skate cooked with paprika and grilled swordfish steaks.

Various cultural groups have influenced the food found here today. The Islamic influence from the Moorish occupation is still strong, in the presence of cumin, saffron and ground nuts and the planting of the olive and orange trees. Chilled soups, barbecued skewered meat, quince paste membrillo and their way of pickling meat continue from the past. Another group to influence the cuisine were the gypsies – stews of beans, vegetables and fruit and dishes of tripe with sausage and chick peas remain. Perhaps the most colourful gypsy dish is huevos flamencos, a mixture of eggs, peppers, prawns and sausages. Andalusia was the first to bring American foods like corn, tomatoes, peppers and potatoes to Europe and Seville is famous for introducing oranges – including the dish duck with orange.

The Mezquita in Cordoba is a Roman Catholic cathedral but the structure was formerly the world's second-largest mosque.

Raw ham with bread is a popular tapa here. These hams can be seen hanging over bars and are cured in the cold sierra air, giving them the name Serrano. The best known of these is jabugo ham. Other traditional Andalusian dishes include the cold vegetable soup gazpacho, bull's tail rabo de toro and delicate dishes of veal.

Various convents in the capital Seville are still making a variety of lovely sweet pastries – a tradition dating back to medieval times. These include yemas, made from egg yolk and sugar and rosquillas rellenas de cidra – cider pastries.

The area around Jerez produces the world's finest sherry. The dry and pale sherry fino is well paired, chilled, with fish and is also used in cooking sauces.

It was Spanish explorers in Mexico who introduced the chilli pepper to Europe and thence to Asia.

Key ingredients of the Spanish kitchen

Before the days of supermarkets and the mass transportation of food, cooks had to make use of local produce and this varied depending on local climate. In Spain, for example, the raw ingredients available in the wet and windy north–west coastal region differed from those on offer in hot, dry Andalusia in the south and this resulted in regional cuisines with their own distinct character. Several mountain ranges dissect the country, too, making transportation and communication more difficult and reinforcing historical regional differences. Foods introduced by invaders, such as the Romans and Moors, or brought back from the New World, further enriched Spain's culinary melting pot.

It is hard to give a shortlist of those ingredients that typify Spanish cuisine across the regions, but the following are just some of the key foodstuffs. The two items that most characterize Spanish cooking are olive oil and garlic – a Roman legacy. Olive oil is used widely in cooking, in marinades and dressings, while the pungent tang of garlic spices many a savoury dish.

Like garlic, onions are essential in Spanish cooking for the tangy flavour they impart to cooked dishes or to salads. Two other vegetables, potatoes and tomatoes – both gifts from the New World – feature in some of Spain's most famous dishes. Potatoes are a key ingredient in tortilla española, or Spanish omelette and in the well-known tapa, patatas bravas. Tomatoes are used in sauces and salads and in Andalusia's famous gazpacho, a cold tomato soup. Eggs are another essential. As well as tortilla española, they are used in a variety of omelets or baked in such dishes as huevos flamencos.

A cornerstone of traditional Spanish gastronomy, Serrano ham is cured for at least a year up in the mountains, then served in wafer-thin slices with such accompaniments as broad beans, in habas con jamôn. Fish and seafood, including squid, prawns, fresh anchovies, fresh sardines and cod, are popular ingredients too – which is not surprising given that Spain has a total of 3,000 miles (5,000 km) of coastline allowing access to both the Mediterranean and Atlantic. Mojama, a type of air-cured tuna and a legacy of the early Arab invaders, is another fishy delicacy.

No discussion of the food of Spain would be complete without a mention of rice, introduced by the Moors who once occupied part of the country. This grain forms the basis of what is probably the most famous Spanish dish of all, paella, as well as other lesser-known recipes. Saffron – another ingredient from Spain's Moorish legacy – is the spice that gives paella rice its characteristic yellow colouring.

Parsley – the flat-leaved variety – is probably the most popular herb. Oregano, thyme and rosemary are used too. Pimenton, Spanish paprika, is a storecupboard essential. It is a characteristic flavouring of chorizo, the spicy sausage made of coarsely chopped pork.

What pasta is to the Italians, bread is to the Spanish. The French-style bread stick known as a barra is served with every meal. It also makes its appearance with tapas and with the merienda, or afternoon snack. To many Spaniards, a meal is not complete without barra.

Olives have been cultivated in Spain for many centuries and the country is now the world's largest producer. Notable varieties include the small brown Arbequina, which is excellent for eating and the Manzanillo – a high-yielding variety which is very widely grown.

Techniques and equipment used in Spanish cooking

A well-equipped modern kitchen should meet most of the needs of anyone wanting to cook Spanish food. However, there are some more specialist pieces of equipment which can be added if liked and which will give a more authentic feel.

The one dish that could be said to characterise Spanish cuisine is the stew known variously, according to the region, as cocido, pote, guiso, estofado, escudella or olla. Olla is also the name for the large casserole dish, wide in the middle and narrow at the top and bottom, which is a classic Spanish cooking utensil.

As well as concocting delicious stews, Spanish cooks also roast, fry and sauté food. Traditionally, the classic Castilian lamb – spread with lard and sprinkled with water – is roasted in a clay dish, but a good set of roasting tins should suffice for most meats. Sturdy, heavy-bottomed (or non-stick) frying pans are essential for cooking tortilla española and other types of omelette, while a deep fryer can be useful for various tapas, such as Andalucia's pescaditos – anchovies and other tiny fish which are coated in batter, then deep-fried – or deep-fried churros which are similar to doughnuts.

Although baking and grilling are not common, the Spaniards do grill meats on a metal plate or cook them over charcoal or an open fire. Available in a variety of materials, the olla – for cooking stews – can also be used over an open fire, as can the earthenware dish known as the cazuela. Available in a wide range of different sizes and infinitely adaptable, it can be placed in the oven, on the hob, on the barbecue or over an open flame and – conveniently – it retains its heat after cooking.

Another favourite barbecued food is sardines. Skewered and grilled over a fire, they are sold along the beachfronts on the Costa del Sol. In Catalonia, the dish known as calçotada – made from calocats, a type of spring onion cooked over an open flame – symbolizes the coming of spring. Traditionally, the spring onions are served on a terracotta roof tile, which keeps them warm. Another dish once cooked over an open fire is Valencia's famous paella. The essential piece of cookware for this is, of course, the round, shallow paellero, or paella pan, in which fideua, a paella made with noodles and fish stock, is also prepared.

Sardines grilling on a Spanish beach.

Every kitchen needs a good selection of knives, but when it comes to carving a Serrano ham, specialist equipment is pretty much essential in what amounts almost to a culinary ritual. A jamônero, or rack, holds the ham in place while it is carved using three razor-sharp knives – a culchillo de jamôn (a special long, flexible knife), a boning knife and a wide-bladed cook's knife.

The mortar and pestle once used for pounding garlic or reducing the ingredients of gazpacho to a purée can, in the modern kitchen, be replaced by the more convenient garlic crusher and blender. A cook's blowtorch or, failing that, the grill, can be used to caramelize the thin, crackly sugar topping of crema Cataläna – Catalonia's version of crème brûlée – instead of the traditional hot iron.

Finally, a small, specially shaped bottle for drizzling olive oil makes a nice touch on the table. As the Spanish say to wish everyone a good meal: buen provecho.

TAPAS

BRAVAS	2.50
CALAMARES	3
SEPIA	2.50
PUNTILLA	3
CROQUETAS	0.50
TELLINAS	3
GAMBAS	4.50
ENSALADILLA	2
JAMON	5
BOQUERONES	2
QUESO	3
TORTILLA	2
CHAMPIÑON	2
PULPO	3

The culture of tapas

Eating tapas is as much part of the Spanish way of life as the traditional siesta. Ranging from simple finger foods like olives or toasted almonds to such cooked dishes as patatas bravas (potatoes in spicy sauce) or tortilla española (Spanish omelette), tapas are snacks taken before the main midday or evening meal. But these delicious appetisers offer a richer experience than the mere consumption of food. They are at the heart of an age-old cultural and social custom that reveals much about the Spanish approach to living and that even has its own vocabulary. The tapeo is the name for the entire activity that surrounds the eating of tapas, while the verb tapear means 'to go out and eat tapas'.

The tapeo begins when Spaniards head for the bars known as tascas (tapas are not served in restaurants or at home). Here they gather to enjoy the company of family and friends, to chat, to gossip, to share a joke and to debate the merits of the local soccer team or the state of the nation, while drinking and snacking. With a glass of wine or sherry (or cider in the north–west) in one hand and a tapa in the other, they build up an appetite for the meal to come – which in the evening can be as late as 10pm – or perhaps even eat so much that they need no further food. The tapeo is very much a moveable feast and participants often stroll from one bar to another. All are welcome to join in, including children.

The credit for the invention of the tapa is usually given to Alfonso X (1221–1284), el Sabio or 'The Wise', ruler of Castile. Once, so the story goes, the king fell ill and during his illness had to take small quantities of food with a little wine between meals, presumably to keep up his strength. On his recovery, he decreed that forthwith wine should never be served in taverns unless accompanied by a snack. His intention was to protect the poor, who could not afford a meal with their wine and so became inebriated when drinking.

There are stories to explain the origin of the name 'tapa' too. After Alfonso's decree was established, tavern-keepers are said to have served wine covered with a slice of smoked ham, cheese, or bread. This 'tapa', meaning 'lid' or 'cover', was both an edible accompaniment to the drink and a way of keeping it free of the dirt, dust or insects that might otherwise fall in.

Another variation on the tale again involves Alfonso X. During a journey through the province of Cádiz, he stopped off at the town of Ventorillo del Chato, where he ordered some sherry, the local fortified wine. Because it was windy, the landlord of the inn covered the royal drink with a slice of ham to protect it from wind-blown dirt. According to the story, the king was so appreciative that when he ordered a second glass, he asked for it to be covered with the same 'tapa' as before.

A more down-to-earth explanation suggests that tapas were invented because farm and other manual workers needed to eat a little during their working hours to keep them going until their proper mealtimes arrived.

Gazpacho, paella, sangria: iconic dishes and drinks

Gazpacho

Gazpacho is a chilled, hearty soup, often thought of as a 'liquid salad', only consumed during Spain's summer months. Gazpacho originates in Andalusia and was originally a combination of stale bread, garlic, olive oil, salt and vinegar. During the Middle Ages, Spanish farmers and shepherds began to throw ripe vegetables into the mix to become a more satisfying meal. After Spain's discovery of the New World, tomatoes and peppers were added to make the gazpacho we know today.

This gradual addition of ingredients and the nature of the dish is reflected in its name. Gazpacho is believed by many to be derived from the word caspa meaning 'fragments' or 'leftovers'. Indeed, there is no single recipe for gazpacho, as Spanish chefs will enthusiastically prepare the tasty soup with whatever vegetable they desire or have to hand. Traditionally, gazpacho was made with a mortar and the ingredients pounded to a paste. Today, blenders take out a lot of the hard work.

Paella

The most notable Spanish dish, the paella, began as a poor man's dish in the eighteenth century and rose to popularity outside of Valencia in the nineteenth century. The Romans introduced the round, shallow, steel pan which was later used to create the dish and the name is derived from the Latin word for pan, patella. The Moors brought rice and saffron to Valencia around this time and the peasants combined these with any other ingredient they could find. Traditionally it included land snails, chicken, rabbit and seasonal vegetables. A later variation saw the addition of seafood and shellfish to paella. After stir-frying meat and vegetables in olive oil, short-grain rice such as calasparra and bomba is spread over the pan in a thin layer and soaks up all the flavours. A previously made stock is added before simmering and finally seasoning. The way to eat paella is communally from the pan, with the dish set in the middle of the table to share joyously with friends and family.

Classic sangria.

Paella valenciana.

Sangría

The light, summer wine punch known as sangría was created to refresh Spain's thirsty bar patrons and is thought of more as a party drink by locals. Originally just made up of red wine and soda water, it was soon combined with chopped fruit, juice and spirits such as brandy or triple sec to make it more appealing. The quality of the punch depends on the freshness of the fruit and flavours of the juice used. Although sangría can sometimes be made with white wine, with various alcoholic potencies and no fixed recipe, it is always easy to drink and served ice-cold from a pitcher or punch bowl. Today, sangría can be found in almost every bar throughout Spain.

The festival of San Fermin, in the Navarrese city of Pamplona, is famous for its bull-running through the streets of the town.

Food and festivals

The best times to be had in Spain are at the many fiestas throughout the year – commemorating patron saints, historic battles, religious holidays and Spanish food itself. Depending on the location and celebration, various treats and feasts will be had by all.

Cooking competitions often provide the food to keep the revellers going throughout the festivities. On the eve of La Tomatina (the world's biggest tomato fight) in Buñol, the town's best cooks hold an unofficial paella contest and during the Fiesta del Arroz (festival of rice) in Sueca, the competition becomes international. Pans of paella are cooked on the streets of Las Fallas (festival of fire) in Valencia to feed the crowds amidst fireworks and flames. During Aste Nagusia (big week) in Bilbao, when the town celebrates its Basque heritage, local chefs compete to produce the best hake in green sauce and cod in garlic sauce. The popular local drink kalimotxo (red wine and cola) is also consumed in large quantities.

At the well-known carnival in Pamplona – the Running of the Bulls – chorizo sausage, Spanish tortilla, thick beef stew and jugs of red wine are all on offer. Chunks of thick country bread help to soak up all the wine. To celebrate the patron saint Virgin Del Rocio of Almonte, snacks of tortilla, jamón, prawns and fried peppers are handed out to the campers and carnival-goers over several days. There's also plenty of local wine and sherry to go around. On the Monday following Easter, a huge picnic occurs on the banks of the River Tormes, where friends and family gather to eat hornazo – a pastry pie filled with ham, sausage, bacon, cooked egg and sometimes chicken.

Particular foods are the sole reason for many Spanish fiestas. Among those celebrated are artichokes in Benicaró, sausages in Requena, cherries in Serra and potatoes and black truffles (on separate days) in Zorita del Maestrazgo. Viver's olive oil festival in Parque de la Floresta features more than 50 of the best oil producers in the region. Requena's grape harvest festival and Jerez's sherry festival are the fiestas for wine lovers. Jerez celebrates the grapes and blessing of the wine – 100 varieties of which are available for tasting. O Grove holds the seafood festival where tasting of all fish–related

Fireworks during the Ferias festival, Salamanca.

dishes is encouraged. Calçotada is the occasion in Valls when massive amounts of calçots (spring onions) are roasted and dipped in salvitxada or romesco sauce and consumed with red wine or cava.

Christmas Eve is the biggest meal of the year in Spain and families eat very well. Usually there will be lobster, roast lamb or suckling pig, fish soup and a wealth of seafood, cheeses, hams and pâtés. A variety of Christmas sweets may follow such as nougats (turron and jijona), marzipan (yema) and crumbly cakes (polvorones and mantecados). Another treat is rosquilloes de vino – biscuits flavoured with anise and wine. No Christmas meal would be complete without walnuts, dates and mandarins. At the pagan festival on Christmas Eve in Baga, Catalonia, the locals eat a savoury cake (coca) with garlic mayonnaise.

CHAPTER 1

Classic Dishes

Galicia
Asturias
Basque
Navarre
La Rioja
Castilla y León
Aragon
Catalonia
Costa Brava
Costa Dorado
MADRID
Costa del Azahar
Extremadura
Castilla La Mancha
Valencia
Balearic Islands
Murcia
Costa Blanca
Andalusia
Costa del Sol

Although Spanish cuisine has a strongly regional quality, the favourite ingredients and cooking techniques are shared across the country, meaning that some dishes have entered a classic repertoire of common foods. These are often straightforward tapas such as salads and grilled fish and dishes based around the staple foods such as breads, pulses and grains. Many desserts, too, fall into this category – regional variation is less pronounced here, with many classic desserts being based around milk, rice and flavourings such as orange, cinnamon and vanilla.

A matador in traditionally ornate dress prepares for a bullfight in Plaza de Toros de Ronda. It is a common misconception that the colour red is supposed to anger the bull – bulls are actually colourblind.

Tortilla española
Spanish potato omelette

Ingredients

2 large potatoes

1 large onion

3 tbsp olive oil

2 cloves garlic, crushed

1 bay leaf

6 large eggs

few drops Tabasco sauce (optional)

salt and freshly ground black pepper

chopped fresh parsley

Serves 6 as a tapa

*S*erved hot or cold, this simple Spanish dish of eggs, onion and potato is a pleasure to eat. Sprinkle with fresh parsley and accompany with some crusty bread and a salad for lunch, or serve up with a piece of toast and coffee for breakfast.

Peel and cut the potatoes into small cubes about 5 mm (¼ inch) thick. Slice the onion into thin shreds.

Heat the oil in a large non-stick frying pan and stir-fry the potatoes, onion and garlic with the bay leaf over a high heat for 5 minutes. Reduce the heat and cook for about 20 minutes, stirring occasionally, taking care not to over brown the mixture.

Meanwhile, whisk together the eggs, Tabasco if using and plenty of seasoning.

Transfer the potato mixture to a 26-cm (10-inch) non-stick frying pan, discard the bay leaf and pour in the beaten eggs. Over a low heat and stirring the set egg from the edge of the pan inwards, cook the mixture for 5 minutes until all the runny egg has begun to set. Pack the mixture down well and continue to cook for a further 5 minutes.

Slide the tortilla on to a plate and return to the frying pan the other way up. Cook gently for a further 5 minutes until set all the way through and golden brown. Serve hot or cold, cut into wedges and sprinkled with the parsley.

Tortilla de guisantes
Green pea tortilla

*T*his variation on the basic tortilla is excellent served in bite-sized pieces with drinks.

Heat the oil in a 23-cm (9-inch) non-stick frying pan. Add the onion, sprinkle with salt and fry gently for about 25 minutes, until tender. Season to taste, then stir in the peas.

Beat the eggs with the mint and salt and pepper, then pour them over the onions and peas. Cook gently for about 10 minutes, pulling away the edges of the tortilla as it sets, to allow the uncooked egg to run underneath.

Meanwhile, preheat the grill. When the tortilla is firm but still moist on top, brown the top under the grill for about 5 minutes, until golden and set. Leave in the pan to cool for a few minutes.

Cover the frying pan with a plate and carefully invert both frying pan and plate. Remove the frying pan. Place another plate on top of the tortilla and invert both plates and tortilla to turn it right-side up. Serve warm or at room temperature, cut into small wedges or bite-size pieces.

Ingredients
2 tbsp olive oil
2 onions, halved and thinly sliced
salt and ground black pepper
275 g (10 oz) frozen peas, thawed
6 eggs
2 tsp chopped fresh mint

Serves 6 as a tapa

Pinchos
Skewered appetisers

*T*hese salty and piquant little skewers – the name means 'thorn' or 'spike' in Spanish – are served with drinks all over Spain. They're the perfect light bite to serve before a big meal.

Roll the anchovies into coils and thread each one onto a separate toothpick. Add a caper and cornichon to each stick and serve.

Ingredients
12 tinned or marinated anchovy
    fillets, drained
12 capers
12 cornichons

Makes 12

Aceitunas aliñadas
Marinated green olives

Green olives marinated in herbs and garlic always seem to be at hand at any Spanish establishment. Served with toasted, salted almonds and often accompanying a frothy beer, these olives especially evoke the taste of Spain.

Lightly crush the olives with a mallet, or make slight slits in each olive with a knife, to ensure that the marinade permeates them. Place the olives in a sealable glass jar and add the remaining ingredients. Fill the jar with water and shake well. Marinate at room temperature for several days to a week.

Serve the olives with toasted almonds and fresh bread.

Ingredients
450 g (1 lb) unpitted green Spanish olives
7 cloves garlic, peeled and minced
2 bay leaves
½ medium lemon, sliced
1 tsp dried oregano
1 tsp ground fennel seeds
½ tsp dried thyme
½ tsp ground cumin
½ tsp dried rosemary
½ tsp Spanish paprika
½ tsp black pepper
toasted almonds, to serve
fresh bread, to serve

Makes 450 g (1 lb)

Ensaladilla
Spanish potato salad

This traditional tapa appears in every region of Spain, with little variation. A poorly made version will taste like a mouthful of mayonnaise. On the other hand, a well-made ensaladilla is a perfectly balanced mixture of potatoes, hard-boiled eggs and vegetables, using the mayonnaise solely to accent these other flavours. This colourful salad is served at nearly every tapas bar; it is even served free at times with an order of beer.

In a saucepan, cook the potatoes and carrot in lightly salted water. Bring to a boil and allow to simmer until almost tender. Fold in the peas and beans and cook until all the vegetables are tender. Drain the vegetables and transfer them to a serving platter. Add the onion, pepper, gherkins, capers, olives and egg slices.

In a separate bowl, thoroughly combine the mayonnaise, lemon juice and mustard. Add this mixture to the serving platter, mixing well to ensure all the ingredients are coated. Sprinkle with pepper and toss. Garnish with chopped parsley and refrigerate. Allow to stand at room temperature for about 1 hour immediately before serving to enhance the salad's flavour. As with any dish made with mayonnaise, ensaladilla should be refrigerated and will not keep for more than 1 to 2 days.

Ingredients

3 medium potatoes
1 large carrot, diced
5 tbsp shelled green peas
100 g (4 oz) green beans
½ medium onion, chopped
1 small red pepper, chopped
4 cocktail gherkins, sliced
2 tbsp baby capers
12 anchovy-stuffed olives
1 hard-boiled egg, thinly sliced
150 ml (5 fl. oz) mayonnaise
1 tbsp lemon juice
1 tsp Dijon mustard
freshly ground black pepper, to taste
chopped fresh parsley, to garnish

Serves 4 as a tapa

Ensalada de cebolla y naranjas
Red onion and orange salad

Ingredients

4 ripe medium oranges, peeled

1 small red onion, finely sliced

2 tbsp raspberry vinegar

6 tbsp extra-virgin olive oil

salt and freshly ground pepper

4 tbsp raisins, soaked for 20 mins in hot water,
    then drained

20 black olives, pitted

2 tbsp sunflower seeds

2 tbsp finely chopped black almonds

sprigs of fresh mint, to garnish

Serves 4 as a tapa

*T*his popular and colourful salad lends a festive note to any tapas table and is featured in many tapas bars throughout Spain. Some versions omit the red onion or replace the raspberry vinegar with lemon juice. No matter which variation is served, however, this salad is tangy and refreshing on a hot summer day and should always be served chilled.

Remove the white pith from the oranges and cut the fruit crosswise into 5-mm (¼-inch) slices. Arrange on a serving platter and scatter over the sliced red onion.

In a small bowl, whisk together the vinegar, olive oil, salt and pepper. Spoon this dressing over the onion and oranges. Sprinkle with the raisins, olives, sunflower seeds and almonds. Garnish with mint sprigs and serve chilled.

Ensalada de cabrales
Frisée and cabrales salad

*T*his salad is simple to prepare and deeply refreshing when the weather is hot: frisée, with its refreshing, slightly bitter flavour; the peppers with their distinctive Mediterranean taste; and the olives and blue cheese, with their pungent, salty bite.

Clean and core the frisée and cut into bite-size pieces. Peel the peppers and cut into strips. Arrange the lettuce in a shallow bowl and garnish with the roasted peppers, blue cheese and green olives. Dress with the olive oil and sherry vinegar. Serve immediately.

Ingredients
1 small head of frisée
2 red peppers, roasted
75 g (3 oz) cabrales or other blue cheese
12 pimento-stuffed green olives
3 tbsp extra-virgin olive oil
1 tbsp sherry vinegar

Serves 4 as a tapa

Cabrales is aged in natural limestone caves, resulting in rich blue veins and a strong, acidic flavour.

Patatas bravas
Crisp spiced potatoes

Ingredients
3 tbsp olive oil, plus extra for frying
2 tbsp finely chopped onion
2 cloves garlic, finely chopped
1½ tbsp Spanish paprika
¼ tsp Tabasco sauce
¼ tsp dried thyme
100 ml (4 fl. oz) ketchup
100 ml (4 fl. oz) mayonnaise
salt and freshly ground black pepper
4 large potatoes, peeled and diced
chopped parsley, to garnish

Serves 4 as a tapa or accompaniment

*P*atatas bravas is a basic, traditional tapa as popular in elegant big-city establishments as it is in the more modest village hostelries. As with most tapas, each bar will have its own recipe, naturally believed to the best! Savour this mildly tangy version of patatas bravas with a chilled white wine.

In a saucepan, heat the 3 tablespoons olive oil over medium heat. Add the onion and garlic and sauté until the onion is soft. Turn off the heat and add the paprika, Tabasco sauce and thyme, stirring well. Transfer to a bowl and add the ketchup and mayonnaise. Season with salt and pepper to taste. Set aside.

Sprinkle the potatoes lightly with salt. In a large frying pan, fry the potatoes in olive oil until cooked through and golden-brown, stirring occasionally. (Take care when adding the potatoes to the saucepan because the oil will splatter due to the salt.) Drain the potatoes on paper towels, check the seasoning, add more salt if necessary and set aside.

Mix the potatoes with the sauce immediately before serving to ensure that the potatoes retain their crispness. Garnish with chopped parsley and serve warm.

Mejillones asados
Grilled mussels

*M*ussels are especially popular along the Bay of Biscay, but they are enjoyed throughout Spain and are delicious cooked in this way. The crust of cheese and breadcrumbs protects the mussels from the fierce heat of the grill, leaving them juicy and full of flavour.

Check the mussels, discarding any that are open or ones that do not close when sharply tapped. Put the closed mussels in a large pan, add 3 tablespoons water, cover tightly and cook over high heat for about 5 minutes, shaking the pan frequently, until the mussels have opened.

Discard any unopened shells. Snap off and discard the top shell of each mussel and arrange the shells with mussels in a flameproof dish.

Preheat the grill. Combine the breadcrumbs, Parmesan cheese, garlic, parsley and oil and season with black pepper. Spoon the crumb mixture onto the mussels, then grill them for about 2 minutes until golden and bubbling. Serve immediately.

Ingredients
500 g (1 lb 2 oz) mussels, cleaned
4 tbsp dry breadcrumbs
3 tbsp freshly grated Parmesan cheese
2 garlic cloves, crushed
2 tbsp chopped fresh parsley
2½ tbsp olive oil
freshly ground black pepper

Serves 4 as a tapa, or 2 as a main course

Gambas en gabardinas
Battered prawns

Ingredients
100 g (4 oz) flour
pinch of salt
3 tbsp oil or melted butter
175 ml (6 fl. oz) tepid water
pinch of cayenne pepper
450 g (1 lb) large prawns in the shell
olive oil for deep frying
1 large egg white
1 lemon, cut into wedges

Serves 4 as a tapa

*T*he light, crisp batter keeps these tender prawns moist in the hot oil.

To make the batter, put the flour and salt in a blender or bowl, work in the oil or butter and add the warm water. Stir to make a smooth batter. Add a pinch of cayenne pepper. Leave this to stand and peel the prawns.

Heat the deep-frying oil to top heat in an electric fryer. Whisk the egg white until it forms soft peaks and fold this into the batter.

Dip each prawn into the batter and drop into the oil. Let the prawns puff up and colour for about 30 seconds, then remove with a slotted spoon onto paper towel. Serve at once with the lemon wedges.

Ensalada de mariscos
Seafood salad

Y̶ou could use any combination of seafood for this salad, but the mixture of scallops, prawns, squid and mussels is particularly rich in flavours and textures.

Fill a large saucepan three-quarters of the way full with water and bring to a boil. Add the lemons, bay leaves, hot sauce and salt. Cook for a few minutes, then add the prawns and cook for about 4 minutes.

Remove the prawns, leaving the cooking water in the pan and immediately transfer the prawns to a bowl of iced water. Bring the cooking water back to a boil and repeat the process with the scallops, cooking for 3 minutes and then the squid, cooking for 1 minute. Add more ice to the water as necessary.

Coat the bottom of a frying pan with olive oil and cook the garlic until it is golden. Add the clams and wine, adding more wine if needed. Cover and steam for 4 minutes, or until the first clams begin to open. Add the mussels and cook until both the clams and mussels open.

Remove the clams and mussels from the pan and set aside, leaving the pan on the heat. Add the thyme to the pan and reduce the stock by three-quarters. Strain and allow to cool to room temperature.

Combine the onion, celery, roasted pepper, basil, 1 tablespoon olive oil and lime juice in a bowl. Cut the prawns and scallops in half and add to the bowl, along with the strained stock. Remove the mussels and clams from the shells and add to the mix. Check for seasoning, adding salt and pepper as needed. Marinate in the refrigerator for at least 30 minutes before serving, garnished with basil leaves.

Ingredients

2 lemons, cut in half
2 bay leaves
½ tsp hot red pepper sauce
salt
225 g (8 oz) prawns, peeled, cleaned and
  deveined
iced water
100 g (4 oz) scallops
3 medium squid, cut into rings
olive oil, for frying, plus 1 tbsp for marinade
2 cloves garlic, sliced
24 clams, cleaned
50 ml (2 fl. oz) white wine, or more if needed
24 mussels, cleaned
¼ bunch thyme, stems removed and finely
  chopped
1 small red onion, finely chopped
1 stalk of celery, finely chopped
1 roasted red pepper, finely chopped
4 fresh basil leaves, finely chopped
½ tsp fresh lime juice
basil leaves, to garnish

Serves 4 as a tapa

Calamares rellenos
Stuffed squid

Ingredients

325 g (12 oz) minced veal

325 g (12 oz) minced pork

1 tsp dried oregano

1 tsp ground cumin

100 ml (4 fl. oz) olive oil

3 whole garlic cloves, peeled

2 medium white onions, finely chopped

1 small green pepper, finely chopped

225 ml (8 fl. oz) dry white wine

225 ml (8 fl. oz) tomato sauce

8 green olives, pitted and sliced

50 g (2 oz) raisins

salt and freshly ground black pepper,

12 extra-large squid tubes, cleaned

toothpicks

1 red pepper, finely chopped

2 garlic cloves, finely chopped

250 g (10 oz) tinned whole tomatoes, crushed
  by hand

1 bay leaf

salad, to serve

fresh parsley, to garnish

Serves 4 as a tapa

S tuffing and stewing is an excellent way to deal with large, slightly tough squid. Instead of tomato sauce, you could serve the squid sprinkled with cheese or accompanied by a dip such as garlic-flavoured mayonnaise.

Thoroughly combine the veal, pork, oregano and cumin in a mixing bowl.

Heat ¼ of the olive oil in a frying pan and, over a medium heat, cook the garlic cloves, 1 onion and the green pepper for about 4 minutes, until soft.

Add the meat mixture, half of the wine and the tomato sauce. Cover and cook over a medium to low heat for about 15 minutes.

Uncover the pan, mix in the olives and raisins and cook for a further 15 minutes, or until the liquid is almost fully reduced, making sure that the meat is still moist. Season with salt and pepper. Remove from the heat and allow to cool.

Stuff the squid with the meat mixture and close the ends with toothpicks. Set aside. Preheat the oven to 180°C (350°F).

Heat the remaining olive oil in a medium saucepan over a medium heat and cook the remaining onion, red pepper and garlic for about 4 minutes, until soft.

Add the tomatoes and the bay leaf and bring the mixture to a boil. Immediately remove from the heat and pour into a 23-cm (9-inch) rectangular baking pan.

Arrange the stuffed squid in the pan and cover with kitchen foil. Bake in the oven for 45 minutes or until the squid are tender. Serve with a side salad and garnish with parsley.

Escabeche de bonito
Pickled tuna

Escabeche is a method of preparing fish in a vinegar- or citrus-based marinade. Sometimes escabeche of chicken, rabbit or pork are served instead of fish. Spain borrowed the technique from the Moors and it has since been exported to Latin America, becoming especially popular in Peru, Mexico and Puerto Rico.

Combine the vinegar, olive oil, onions, pepper, capers, paprika and olives in a mixing bowl. Set aside.

Heat the olive oil in a frying pan and cook the tuna and garlic for 2 minutes on each side. Set aside.

Add the marinade and cook for 4 minutes. Remove from the heat and season with salt and pepper. Place in the refrigerator and marinate overnight before serving, garnished with lemon wedges.

Ingredients

4 tbsp white wine vinegar
175 ml (6 fl. oz) extra virgin olive oil
2 medium white onions, finely sliced
1 medium green pepper, finely sliced
50 g (2 oz) capers
½ tsp paprika
10 large green olives, pitted
   and sliced
2 tbsp olive oil
1.5 kg (3 lb) fresh tuna, cleaned, deboned and
   cut into 1-inch slices
2 garlic cloves, finely sliced
salt and freshly ground black pepper
lemon wedges, to garnish

Serves 4

Ceviche de gambas
Prawn salad

Ingredients

900 g (2 lb) prawns or 450 g (1 lb) prawns
  and 450 g (1 lb) white fish
1 litre (2 pints) water
600 ml (20 fl. oz) lime juice
2 medium red onions,
  finely chopped
2 tbsp soy sauce
salt and freshly ground
  black pepper
2 cucumbers, cubed
1 red pepper, deseeded and cubed
1 bunch fresh dill, chopped
Tabasco sauce, to taste
lime wedges, to serve

Serves 8 as a tapa

*T*his salad is bursting with fresh flavours, combining sweet prawns with a herby, salty–sour dressing. The prawns are not cooked – though they look and taste it – so you must buy the very freshest.

Shell and devein the prawns and skin and clean fish if using. Place in a large bowl.

Mix the ingredients for the marinade together (water, lime juice, red onions, soy sauce, salt and pepper) and pour over the prawns. Marinate for 20 minutes.

Add the cucumber, pepper cubes and dill. Toss together in the bowl.

Spoon onto plates or into small bowls. Sprinkle with pepper and Tabasco sauce. Serve with lime wedges.

Camarones al ajillo
Garlic prawns

*T*his recipe is packed with garlic, so you may wish to reduce the quantities. It is based on a Spanish peasant dish made with plump, fresh prawns, and is simple but extremely tasty. Serve with plenty of bread to mop up the juices.

Remove the heads from the prawns, but do not peel. Wash and pat dry the prawns and place in a shallow glass dish. Add the lime juice and oregano. Cover and chill for 2 hours.

When ready to cook, heat 2 tablespoons of the olive oil in a frying pan and gently fry the garlic for 1 minute, stirring, making sure it does not burn.

Raise the heat and add the prawns with the marinating juices and the remaining olive oil. Stir-fry for 5 minutes until the prawns are pink all over, then season with the salt and black pepper.

Pile the prawns onto warmed plates, sprinkle with the parsley and serve with the wedges of lime and some crusty bread.

Ingredients
900 g (2 lb) raw extra-large prawns
juice of 2 limes, plus lime wedges to garnish
½ tsp dried oregano
6 tbsp extra-virgin Spanish olive oil
8 cloves garlic, finely chopped
salt and freshly ground black pepper
2 tbsp chopped fresh parsley

Serves 4 as a tapa

Merluza española
Spanish-style haddock

Ingredients
450 g (1 lb) haddock fillet or similar white fish, skinned
3 tbsp fruity olive oil
1 small onion, finely sliced
2 cloves garlic, finely sliced
100 g (4 oz) sliced mushrooms
1 small red pepper, deseeded and sliced
1 small green pepper, deseeded and sliced
salt and freshly ground black pepper
100 ml (4 fl. oz) white wine vinegar
75 ml (3 fl. oz) water
1 tbsp sugar

Serves 4 as a light main dish

Serve with crusty bread for a summer lunch or light supper.

Cut the fish into bite-size pieces. Heat 2 tablespoons of the oil in a frying pan and fry the fish until just cooked. Transfer it to a glass dish. Heat the remaining oil in the frying pan; add the onion and garlic and cook until soft but not browned. Stir in the mushrooms and peppers and cook for a further 1–2 minutes – the vegetables should retain a crisp texture. Spoon the vegetables over the fish and season lightly.

Pour the vinegar and water into the frying pan and bring to a boil. Stir in the sugar until dissolved, then pour the liquid over the fish and vegetables. Leave to cool, then cover and place in the refrigerator for 24 hours.

The Plaza de la Esperanza fish market in Santander, Cantabria.

Cangrejos de rio con tomate
Freshwater crayfish in tomato sauce

Crayfish served with a simple, fresh tomato sauce make a delicious treat of an appetiser. You could use other shellfish, such as crab or lobster, if you prefer.

Heat about 3 tablespoons of the olive oil in a large, deep frying pan. Fry the onions and garlic in the oil until the onion is soft and translucent. While the onions and garlic are cooking, chop the tomatoes finely. Add the wine and the rest of the oil to the frying pan, along with the tomatoes and their juice. Sprinkle in a pinch of cayenne pepper. Simmer for about 10 minutes, stirring often, until the sauce has thickened slightly. Season to taste. Keep warm while you cook the crayfish.

Bring plenty of water to a boil in a large saucepan. Add the live crayfish to the boiling water and cook until they turn red. Remove the pan from the heat and drain.

Add the crayfish to the frying pan with the tomato sauce and stir well, coating the crayfish thoroughly with the sauce.

Ingredients
4 tbsp olive oil
1 onion, finely chopped
3 large cloves garlic, finely chopped
4 large tomatoes
pinch cayenne pepper
900 g (2 lb) live crayfish
175 ml (6 fl. oz) white wine
salt and freshly ground pepper

Serves 2 as a main course or 4 as a tapa

Croquetas de jamón
Ham croquettes

Ingredients
olive oil for frying
1.5 kg (3 lb) smoked ham, chopped
1 onion, chopped
2 red bell peppers, chopped
2 garlic cloves, sliced
2 tbsp tomato paste
4 tbsp fresh chopped parsley
½ tsp freshly grated nutmeg
100 ml (4 fl. oz) double cream
100 g (4 oz) plain flour
salt and freshly ground black pepper
2 eggs, lightly beaten
225 g (8 oz) coarse breadcrumbs
vegetable oil, for frying

Makes 6–8

*C*roquettes, originally from France, long ago became a delicacy and favourite snack throughout the Spanish-speaking world. This is a typical Iberian recipe. You could replace the smoked ham with cooked, shredded chicken.

Heat the olive oil in a large frying pan and cook the ham, onion, peppers and garlic for about 8 minutes. Stir in the tomato paste and cook until it caramelizes. Add the parsley, nutmeg and heavy cream. Sprinkle in 50 g (2 ounces) of the flour and season with salt and pepper. Let the mixture cool to room temperature.

Put the mixture through a meat grinder, or grind in a food procesor. Shape the mixture into finger-shaped sticks, or small patties.

Coat the croquetas by first dipping them into the remaining flour, then the eggs and finally into the breadcrumbs.

Pour vegetable oil into a frying pan to a depth of 2.5 cm (1 inch) and heat to medium – 375°F (190°C) on a frying thermometer, or until a cube of bread dropped in turns golden brown in 60 seconds. Fry the croquetas until golden brown.

Arroz amarillo
Spanish rice

*R*ice has been grown in Valencia since it was brought to Iberia by the Moors in the tenth century. The supreme Spanish crops are calasparra and bomba, both short-grained rices which retain their shape in cooking without gaining creamy soft edges – making them ideal for paella and other dishes. Any white rice can be used to good effect in this simple, traditional Spanish preparation.

Ingredients
4 tbsp olive oil
1 large onion, peeled and diced
775 g (1¾ lb) white rice
1.5 litres (2½ pints) water
salt
2 bay leaves
¼ tsp turmeric

Serves 6 as an accompaniment

Heat the olive oil in a medium saucepan over a medium heat. Add the onion and cook until soft. Add the rice, stirring, until coated with the oil.

Add the water and bring to a boil. Season generously with salt and add the bay leaves and turmeric. Cook over a medium heat, uncovered, for about 20 minutes, until most of the water has been absorbed by the rice.

Churros

Spanish doughnuts

Ingredients

200 g (7 oz) self-raising flour
2 tbsp caster sugar
¼ tsp salt
4 tbsp olive oil
175 ml (6 fl. oz) water
1 egg, beaten
oil for deep frying
icing sugar, for dusting

Serves 4

*C*hurros are long thin strips of fluted dough formed into loops and fried. If thicker and straight, they are called porras, and if in the shape of a ring or hollow ball, buñuelos.

Sift the flour, sugar and salt together onto a plate. Set aside. In a saucepan, bring the oil and water to a boil. Remove from the heat and quickly add the flour mixture. Beat vigorously until smooth. Gradually beat in the egg until the mixture forms a smooth, thick paste.

Half-fill a large, deep frying pan suitable for deep-frying with oil and heat to 190°C (375°F), or until a cube of bread dropped into the oil turns golden brown in 60 seconds. Spoon the dough into a pastry bag fitted with a 1-cm (½-inch) nozzle and pipe 3 or 4 pieces of dough into the hot oil, using the nozzle to form the dough into spirals or horseshoe shapes. Fry for 2–3 minutes or until golden. Using a slotted spoon, transfer the dough pieces to paper towels and drain.

Fry the remaining mixture in the same way. Generously dust all the fried pastries with icing sugar and serve hot with coffee or hot chocolate.

Arroz con leche
Rice pudding

*T*his simple milk-based pudding has become popular across the Spanish-speaking world. A delicious variation from Argentina and Uruguay is to serve it with a spoonful of dulce de leche.

Combine the rice, water, salt, lemon rind and cinnamon sticks in a medium saucepan and cook over a medium heat for about 15 minutes.

Once the rice begins to split open, add the evaporated milk and sugar. Cook over a very low heat, stirring continuously, until the mixture becomes creamy. Remove and reserve the cinnamon sticks.

Remove from the heat and add the vanilla. Chill in individual serving cups and serve sprinkled with ground cinnamon and the reserved cinnamon sticks.

Ingredients
90 g (3½ oz) white long-grain rice, rinsed
450 ml (¾ pint0 water
½ tsp salt
rind of 1 lemon, grated
3 cinnamon sticks
275-g (10-oz) tin evaporated milk
200 g (7 oz) caster sugar
1 tsp vanilla extract
ground cinnamon, to garnish

Serves 4

Dulce de cascaras
Candied citrus rind

Ingredients
3 large ripe grapefruit
water
salt
400 g (14 oz) superfine sugar
1 litre (1¾ pints) water
cream cheese, to serve

Serves 6–8

Candying your own rind makes you realize how poorly shop-bought rind imitates the real thing. This is a delicious dessert, especially if the acid flavour is softened by serving it with something creamy and slightly sweet, such as cream cheese.

Quarter and peel the grapefruits, being sure to remove as much of the bitter white pith as possible. Cover the shells in cold, salted water for 24 hours, changing the water regularly to remove bitterness.

The following day, drain the shells and discard the soaking water. Place the grapefruit shells in a large saucepan with fresh, cold water to cover and bring to the boil over a medium to high heat. Discard the water as soon as it reaches boiling point and repeat the procedure.

Drain the shells and pat them dry with paper towels to remove all the moisture. Place them in a large saucepan with the sugar and water and cook over a low heat, uncovered, until the shells are soft and transparent and the syrup has thickened, for about 1½–2 hours.

Leave the shells and syrup to cool to room temperature. Transfer them to a bowl and refrigerate, covered, until ready to serve. Serve chilled with cream cheese.

Natillas de chocolate
Chocolate pudding

*N*atillas is a generic name for a type of Spanish custard dish. This chocolate version is creamy, sweet and comforting.

Place the milk, cinnamon and salt in a saucepan and bring to a boil. Remove from the heat and set aside.

Beat the egg yolks and sugar in a mixing bowl. In a separate bowl, thoroughly dissolve the flour in the water and add to the yolk mixture. Add the boiled milk and then strain into a saucepan. Place the mixture over a medium heat and add the chocolate, stirring constantly, until the chocolate melts and the mixture becomes thick. Stir in the vanilla.

Pour into bowls, let cool to room temperature and chill until ready to serve. Serve with a little whipped cream and decorate with slivered cinnamon sticks.

Ingredients
2.4 litres (4 pints) milk
1 cinnamon stick
¼ teaspoon salt
8 medium egg yolks
275 g (10 oz) sugar
4 tbsp plain flour
50 ml (2 fl. oz) water
225 g (8 oz) milk chocolate
1 tsp vanilla extract
whipped cream, to serve
cinnamon sticks, to decorate

Serves 10

Compota de peras
Pear compôte

Ingredients
900 g (2 lb) pears
juice ½ lemon
225 g (8 oz) caster sugar
450 ml (¾ pint) water
1 cinnamon stick

Serves 4

*P*ears usually thrive in cool, temperate locations and are thought to have originated in the foothills of a mountain range in western China. But they are widely cultivated in Spain and are popular in simple desserts such as this one.

Peel and core the pears and cut each one into about six pieces. Place in a saucepan and quickly sprinkle lemon juice over them to prevent discolouration. Add the sugar, water and cinnamon stick to the pan and bring to a boil. Simmer for 10–15 minutes, until the pears are very soft but still hold their shape. Serve warm or at room temperature, heaped into glasses with some of the cooking syrup.

Sangría tradicional
Basic sangría

A very simple, unfussy sangría. While this sangría is delicious as it is, this recipe intentionally leaves ample room for improvisation and additions and should therefore be used as a springboard to create your own unique sangría recipes. The unaltered recipe below, however, would meet with the approval of strict sangría traditionalists.

In a large punch bowl or serving jug, combine all ingredients except the sparkling water, mixing well. Refrigerate overnight. Immediately before serving, mix in the sparkling water for added fizz. Ladle into cups with ice cubes.

Ingredients
750 ml (1¼ pints) dry red wine
1 tbsp sugar
juice of 1 large orange
juice of 1 large lemon
1 large orange, sliced thin crosswise
1 large lemon, sliced thin crosswise
2 medium peaches, peeled, stoned and cut
    into chunks
225 ml (8 fl. oz) sparkling water
ice cubes, to serve

Makes 4 glasses

Sangría blanca
White sangría

*B*ursting with sparkling flavour, this clear version of sangría is unique in its use of ice cubes made from apple juice. For parties, this can be served in a large, transparent punch bowl next to a transparent bowl containing traditional red sangría. This pairing provides a beautiful contrast, provided they are not immediately consumed by eager guests, as is often the case.

To make the apple-juice ice cubes, pour the apple juice into two ice trays and freeze until the sangría is ready to serve.

Combine the water, mint, sugar and cinnamon in a saucepan and bring to the boil over medium heat. Reduce the heat and simmer for several minutes. Remove from the heat and leave to cool to room temperature. Remove and discard the mint and cinnamon sticks. Transfer the remaining mixture to a large serving bowl.

Add the wine, peaches, pears and the orange and lemon slices to the serving bowl. Mix well, cover and refrigerate overnight. Immediately before serving, mix in the sparkling apple cider and the apple-juice ice cubes. Decorate with fresh mint leaves, if desired.

Ingredients

apple juice, for ice cubes
300 ml (10 fl. oz) water
1 small bunch fresh mint
90 g (3½ oz) sugar
3 cinnamon sticks
750 ml (1¼ pints) dry white wine
2 medium peaches, peeled, pitted and sliced
2 small pears, cut into chunks
2 medium oranges, sliced crosswise
2 small lemons, sliced crosswise
750 ml (1¼ pints) sparkling apple cider
mint leaves, to decorate (optional)

Makes 8 glasses

CHAPTER 2

Northern Spain

SANTANDER

⊙ OVIEDO

Asturias

Cantabria

⊙ SANTIAGO DE
COMPOSTELA

Galicia

Galicia, in the north–western tip of the
Iberian peninsula, feels very remote from
the rest of Spain. It has preserved its dense forests
and beautiful fjord-like estuaries, called rías, and
is often windswept and rainy. Unsurprisingly, fish
dominates the cuisine of this coastal region. Further
east, Asturias is the centre of Spain's mining country.
It is famed for its excellent apples and milk, as well
as the bean dish called fabada. Cantabria is the
mountainous corridor between the Basque Country
and the rest of Spain, with its culture centred on the
casino city of Santander and a cuisine based around
nourishing dishes of game, beans and fish.

*Fishing boats in a Galician harbour. Sea-fishing remains a major industry along Spain's northern coast. The
region of Galicia is sometimes referred to as the 'costa do morisco' – seafood coast – by its inhabitants.*

Caldo gallego
Galician bean, pork and greens soup

*T*raditionally this is a spring soup, made with the tender leaves of young spring turnips and a special variety of new potatoes, called cachelos. The flavour is enriched by the use of salt meat. Use spare ribs or salted pork belly, whichever is most readily available.

If using pork ribs, rub them well with salt. Alternatively, salt pork must be blanched. Put it with the ham hock (gammon knuckle) in a saucepan, cover with cold water and bring to a boil. Simmer for 5 minutes, then drain. Cube the pork.

Drain the beans and put them, with the meat and bones, into an ovenproof dish. Add 2 litres (3¼ pints) water, bring to a simmer, and skim off any scum. Cook gently, covered, for an hour.

Add the potatoes and simmer until done. Remove all bones from the pot and taste the stock. Season with salt and pepper as necessary. Add the greens and simmer for 5–10 minutes. Remove all meat from the bones and return the meat to the pan. To thicken the liquid a little, mash in a few of the potatoes.

Ingredients

250 g (9 oz) dried haricot beans, soaked overnight
325 g (¾ lb) pork belly ribs or 100 g (4 oz) salt pork
salt and freshly ground black pepper
450 g (1 lb) smoked ham hock (gammon knuckle)
450 g (1 lb) new potatoes
200 g (7 oz) tender turnip leaves or kale

Serves 6

The cathedral of Santiago de Compostela – the capital of Galicia. It is here that the Feast of Saint James, one of the biggest Spanish fiestas in the Christian calendar, takes place annually.

Sopa de castañas
Creamy chestnut soup

Ingredients
450 g (1 lb) chestnuts
salt and freshly ground black pepper
1 thick slice bread
4 tbsp olive oil
2 tbsp red wine vinegar
750 ml (1¼ pints) light stock
⅛ tsp cinnamon

Serves 4

In Galicia, chestnuts are often used where beans or potatoes might be used in the rest of Europe. They are softened by the paprika-flavoured juices of fried sausages, or heaped round roast pork or duck. Here they make a creamy winter soup, lightly spiced with a hint of cinnamom.

Slash the chestnut shells across the fat part of each nut. Drop the nuts into a saucepan and cover them with salted cold water. Bring to the boil and simmer for 30 minutes. Leave to cool without removing from the water. Peel the chestnuts and remove the brown skins. Chop them coarsely.

Fry the bread in the oil, then put it in a blender or food processor and purée with the vinegar. Reserve a handful of the chopped chestnuts to add texture to the soup. Add the rest to the blender, a little at a time, with some of the stock. Purée to a cream. Flavour discreetly with cinnamon. Add the reserved chopped chestnuts, heat through, and serve.

Empanadas
Galician stuffed pastries

*E*mpanadas are most often associated with Latin America—but in fact, these crisp and tasty turnovers originated in Galicia.

Preheat the oven to 175°C (350°F). Heat the oil in a large frying pan. When the oil is hot, add the chopped onions and fry for 3 minutes, until the onions are translucent. Add both paprikas, red pepper flakes, cumin, and vinegar and stir until well combined. Add the minced beef and cook until the meat is browned. Drain half the fat from the pan. On a lightly floured surface, roll out the puff pastry 0.5 cm (¼ inch) thick. Using a 13-cm (5-inch) cutter, cut out circles of pastry. One packet of puff pastry should yield 8 rounds.

Using a pastry brush, glaze the top edge of each circle with water. Spoon 2 tablespoons of the filling onto the lower half of the circle. Sprinkle each with raisins and olives. Fold the top half of the circle over, pressing the edges to seal. Crimp the edge by twisting the pastry inward, from one side to the other. This will prevent the juices from leaking during baking. Glaze the tops of the empanadas with the egg. Prick the crust with a fork near the seam to allow steam to escape. Place the empanadas on a baking sheet lined with baking parchment and bake for 25 minutes, or until the filling is hot and the crust is golden.

Ingredients

2 tbsp olive oil
2 medium onions, chopped
2 tsp smoked sweet paprika
½ tsp hot paprika
½ tsp crushed red pepper flakes
1 tsp ground cumin
1 tbsp white vinegar
450 g (1 lb) lean minced beef
450 g (1 lb) puff pastry, defrosted if frozen
50 g (2 oz) raisins
100 g (4 oz) pitted green olives, chopped
1 large egg, lightly beaten

Makes 8

Empanadillas de atún y de queso
Tuna and goat's cheese empanadillas

*E*mpanadillas, the smaller, pocket-size versions of empanadas, are generally served as tapas. Because they can be eaten with the hands, they are perfect snack or party food.

Heat the olive oil in a frying pan over medium heat. Add the onion and garlic and sauté for about 5 minutes or until softened. Remove from the heat and set aside. Using a fork, mash the tuna with the onion, garlic, goat's cheese, olives, pine nuts, capers, paprika, salt and pepper. Set aside.

On a floured surface, roll out the pastry to 3-mm (⅛-inch) thickness. Using a 7.5-cm (3-inch) biscuit cutter, cut out as many dough circles as the dough will allow, rerolling the dough sheets if necessary. Cupping each dough round in your hand, spoon about 1 teaspoon of the filling into the centre of it, then brush the edges with a little water. Fold the dough over the mixture to form a crescent. Pinch the edges of crescent to seal the dough closed. Use the back of a fork to further press the edges of the dough together.

Transfer to a greased baking sheet, and repeat the process with the remaining dough rounds and pastry. Bake in the oven at 200°C (400°F) for 20–25 minutes or until golden. Allow to cool for 5 minutes before serving.

Ingredients
1 tbsp olive oil
5 tbsp minced onion
2 cloves garlic, minced
175 g (6 oz) tinned tuna, packed in olive oil
100 g (4 oz) goat's cheese
75 g (3 oz) pimento-stuffed olives, chopped
5 tbsp toasted pine nuts
5 tbsp capers, chopped
1 tsp paprika
salt and pepper, to taste
450 g (1 lb) puff pastry, defrosted if frozen

Serves 6–8

Paella de salchicha y venera
Galician sausage and scallop paella

*G*alicia is famous throughout Spain for the extraordinary quality of its seafood. Due to its exposed position on the north-western tip of Spain, Galicia has an inordinately large number of fish available to it. In fact, Galician fishermen bring in more scallops each year than anywhere else in Spain. With a nod towards Galicia, this paella teams scallops with prawns and sausage to lend the rice a rich, tender flavour. Enjoy this dish with a chilled glass of Galician wine, such as Albariño.

Heat the olive oil in a paella pan over medium heat. Add the onion and cook for 5 minutes. Throw in the pepper and cook for a further 5 minutes. Add the garlic and continue to cook for about a further 3 minutes. Add the sausage and cook for about 8 minutes, or until done.

Mix in the rice and sauté for about a further 5 minutes. Pour in the stock and saffron and cook for a further 15 minutes. Add the wine, scallops, prawns, peas, tomatoes, salt and pepper. Continue cooking for 8 minutes or until the liquid has been absorbed and the rice is tender. Taste for seasoning, and serve at once.

Ingredients
50 ml (2 fl. oz) olive oil
1 medium yellow onion, chopped
1 large red pepper, chopped
2 cloves garlic, minced
225 g (8 oz) Kielbasa sausage, skinned and chopped
625 g (1 lb 6 oz) rice
1.3 litres (2¼ pints) fish stock
½ tsp saffron
100 ml (4 fl. oz) dry white wine
225 g (8 oz) scallops
325 g (12 oz) uncooked prawns, peeled and deveined
275 g (10 oz) frozen peas, defrosted
3 medium tomatoes, peeled, deseeded and chopped
salt and white pepper, to taste

Serves 6 as a main course, 8–10 as a tapa

Pulpo a la gallega
Galician-style octopus

Ingredients

one 6- to 8-lb octopus
4.5 litres (1 gallon) water, salted
1 lemon, cut in half
1 medium white onion, peeled
  and cut in half
2 bay leaves
1 bunch fresh parsley, stems left whole and
  leaves chopped
2 tbsp hot red pepper sauce
2 medium baking potatoes, washed
50 ml (2 fl. oz) olive oil
3 cloves garlic, peeled and sliced
½ medium white onion, finely sliced
3 tsp paprika
salt and fresh ground black pepper, to season

Serves 4 as a tapa

*T*his tender stewed octopus dish is the signature meal of Galicia. If octopus are not easily available, you could substitute squid. But be sure to use large squid: the tender baby ones are not suited to this long, slow cooking.

Hold the octopus by the tentacles and bang it against the countertop several times to tenderise it. Combine the water, lemon halves, onion halves, bay leaves, whole parsley stems, hot sauce and octopus in a large saucepan and bring to a boil over a high heat. Cook for about 1½ hours or until the octopus is tender. During the last 30 minutes, add the potatoes.

Remove the potatoes and set aside. Leave to cool to room temperature. Remove the octopus and leave to cool for a few minutes.

Peel the octopus, which must be done while it is still hot, and completely remove all the ink and the suction cups. Do not rinse the octopus during this process. Keep a bowl of ice water nearby to use to cool your hands. Cut the peeled octopus into 2.5-cm (1-inch) pieces and set aside.

Peel the potatoes and cut into 5-cm (2-inch) cubes. Heat the olive oil in a medium frying pan and cook the garlic over a medium heat. Add the onion, potatoes and octopus. Add the paprika and chopped parsley. Mix well and season with salt and pepper.

Vieiras de Santiago
Saint James's baked scallops

*E*very restaurant in the old town of Santiago offers this dish on Saint James's Day, for scallops have always been associated with this saint and scallop shells are still the badge of the many pilgrims who visit his shrine. Galician scallops are huge, and benefit from the robust flavours of brandy and tomato which make up this sauce.

Heat the butter and 1 tablespoon of oil and quickly fry the scallops for 2 minutes on each side. Shelled or defrosted scallops make a lot of liquid, so remove them when cooked, then boil this off.

Warm the brandy in a ladle, flame it, and pour over the scallops. Then spoon them into upper scallop shells or small heatproof dishes.

Add another 2 tablespoons of oil to the pan and fry the onion gently, adding the garlic as it softens. Add the chopped tomatoes, paprika and cayenne pepper, and cook until the mixture has reduced to a sauce. Add the wine, then salt and pepper to taste, and spoon over the scallops.

Mix the breadcrumbs and parsley and sprinkle thinly on top of the scallops. Heat through for 2–3 minutes under a low grill and serve immediately.

Ingredients

1 tbsp butter
3 tbsp olive oil
400 g (14 oz) shelled scallops
4 tbsp brandy
1 onion, finely chopped
3 garlic cloves, finely chopped
200 g (7 oz) ripe tomatoes, skinned
    and deseeded
1 tsp paprika
pinch of cayenne pepper
100 ml (4 fl. oz) dry white wine
salt and freshly ground black peppper
3 tbsp fine breadcrumbs
1 tbsp chopped fresh parsley

Serves 4 as a tapa

Fabada asturiana
Bean and sausage pot

Ingredients

725 g (1 lb 10 oz) dried white beans

boiling water

675 g (1½ lb) salt pork belly (or salt brisket)

675 g (1½ lb) ham hocks

6 black peppercorns, crushed

1 tsp paprika

pinch of powdered saffron

1 bay leaf

2 tbsp oil (optional)

4 garlic cloves, chopped

450 g (1 lb) chorizo or other smoked sausage

175 g (6 oz) morcilla or other blood sausage

Serves 6 as a main course

*I*n Asturias, this beanpot is flavoured with local specialities such as lacon, the cured front leg of a pig. Salt pork and cured beef make good substitutes. Cured sausages are also added, giving an incredible richness to the flat, white beans.

Choose a saucepan that holds at least 6 litres (10 pints). Cover the beans, in a bowl, with plenty of boiling water. Put the salt meat into the pan and cover with cold water. Bring to a boil, then drain the meat and return to the saucepan. Drain the beans and add them to the pan with the peppercorns, paprika, saffron and bay leaf. Add 2.5 litres (4 pints) water. Bring slowly to the boil, then simmer very gently, over minimum heat, for 2 hours. Check occasionally that the beans are still covered, but do not stir or they will break up.

Remove the meat and leave it to cool a little. Strip off the skin and fat and take about 2 tablespoons of chopped fat for frying (or use oil). Sweat the fat in a frying pan. Fry the garlic lightly in the melted fat, then spoon it into the beans.

Slice the chorizo and morcilla and fry them until cooked through. Stir into the saucepan, along with their melted fat. Remove all the meat from the ham hock. Chop it, and the salt pork or beef, and return the meat to the saucepan. Simmer for a few minutes. Check the seasonings and serve.

Habitas refritas
Refried kidney beans

*T*he translation of this recipe as 'refried' can cause confusion, as it is often interpreted as 'fried again'. In fact, the Spanish term refrito is actually a reference to overfrying the mashed beans so that they dry out enough to retain a shape in which they can be served.

Place the first 7 ingredients in a saucepan, bring to a boil, and simmer for 40 minutes.

Place one-quarter of the mixture in a food processor and purée. Remix the puréed beans with the whole beans.

Chop the bacon and place in boiling water for 10 minutes to remove the saltiness. Remove from the water and drain.

Heat the butter in a frying pan and fry the bacon. Add the beans, little by little, and mash with the back of a spoon. Season well.

The beans should turn into a thick purée. Season, sprinkle with parsley and serve. The more often you refry the beans, the better they taste.

Ingredients
450-g (1-lb) tin kidney beans
1 red chilli, deseeded and chopped
1 medium onion, finely chopped
2 tsp garlic, crushed
1 tsp paprika
salt and freshly ground
   black pepper
1 litre (2 pints) water
6 rashers bacon, without the rind
60 g (2¼ oz) butter
parsley, to garnish

Serves 2–4 as an accompaniment

Leche frita
Crisp custard squares

Ingredients

500 ml (18 fl. oz) full-cream milk

3 strips lemon zest

½ cinnamon stick

100 g (4 oz) caster sugar, plus extra
  for dusting

4 tbsp cornflour

2 tbsp plain flour

3 large egg yolks

sunflower oil, for frying

2 eggs, to coat

6 tbsp breadcrumbs

ground cinnamon, for dusting

Serves 6

This recipe, popular throughout northern Spain, combines a meltingly creamy centre with a crunchy coating. The squares can be enjoyed hot or cold.

Bring the milk, lemon zest, cinnamon stick and sugar to a boil in a saucepan, stirring gently. Cover and remove from the heat to infuse for 20 minutes.

Put the cornflour and plain flour in a bowl and beat in the egg yolks with a wooden spoon. Start adding some of the milk until the batter is smooth. Strain in the rest of the hot milk, then pour back into the pan. Cook over a low heat, stirring continuously. It will not curdle, but does thicken unevenly if you let it. Cook for a couple of minutes until it becomes a thick custard that separates from the side of the pan. Beat it hard with the spoon to keep it smooth. Pour into a small baking tray, smoothing to a square about 20 cm x 20 cm (8 x 8 inches) and 2.5 cm (1 inch) deep. Cool and then chill.

Pour oil into a shallow frying pan to a depth of about 1 cm (½ inch) and heat until very hot. Cut the custard into 12 squares. Beat the eggs on a plate and lift half the squares into the egg with a metal spatula. Coat and then lift them onto a tray of crumbs (big stale crumbs are best, but dried will do) and coat all round.

Using a clean palette knife, transfer the squares to the pan and fry for a couple of minutes, spooning the oil over the top, until golden. Drain on kitchen paper while you fry the second batch. Dust with sugar and cinnamon before serving. They can be served hot, but are excellent when chilled.

Carajitos
Hazelnut macaroons

*N*ut *bushes are a key part of the northern Spanish landscape, so it is not surprising that excellent nuts are used to make the best biscuits. Children eat these hazelnut macaroons with a glass of milk at the end of the afternoon.*

Toast the nuts in the oven while it heats to 190°C (375°F). Grind them in a food processor. Do not over-grind or they will become very oily.

Rub some sugar over the grater to pick up leftover lemon oil, then rub the zest thoroughly into all the sugar. Sprinkle with cinnamon.

Whisk the egg whites until they form soft peaks. Stir about a quarter of the egg white into the ground nuts to soften them. Sprinkle about half the sugar over the whites and gently fold in, then fold in the remainder alternately with the nut mixture.

Dot walnut-size pieces onto greased foil on 1 or 2 baking sheets, pressing them out gently and spacing them 2.5 cm (1 inch) apart. Bake for 15 minutes until golden brown. Let cool for 5 minutes, then remove from the foil.

Ingredients
150 g (5 oz) blanched hazelnuts
150 g (5 oz) caster sugar
finely grated zest ½ lemon
pinch ground cinnamon
2 large egg whites
butter, for greasing

Makes about 20

CHAPTER 3

The Pyrenees

The Pyrenees divide the Iberian peninsula from the rest of Europe. There are few passes across the mountains and those which are to be found are at high altitudes. Geography has conspired to isolate some communities sheltered by the mountains, protecting local cultures such as – most famously – the Basque people. The other Pyrenean regions in Spain's north-east (Catalonia, Aragon, La Rioja and Navarre) share with the Basque Country a reputation for serving some of the finest food in the peninsula. Catalonia has so many dishes that it warrants a separate chapter; but Aragon and Navarre contribute many recipes to this section, notably those featuring the region's favourite ingredients – fish, seafood and lamb.

The Mallos de Riglos rock formations form part of the foothills of the Pyrenees. Rugged terrain and spectacular natural beauty are par for the course in this part of Spain.

Asadilla
Baked salad of red pepper and tomato

*T*he name of this recipe means 'little baked vegetables'.
This vibrantly red salad is a Spanish summer favourite.
Try serving it with lightly toasted crusty bread, or decorate
with strips of anchovy fillet.

If you have a gas hob, hold the peppers on a carving fork in the flame until black and blistered. Otherwise grill them, giving them a quarter turn every 5 minutes. Put them in a plastic bag for 10 minutes, then strip off the skins. Pull out the stems and discard the seeds, but keep the juice.

Meanwhile skin and quarter the tomatoes. Turn their seeds and juice into a small jug. Slice the flesh lengthwise into strips and put into an oiled baking dish. Slice the peppers the same way and mix in. Sprinkle with the garlic, marjoram, remaining oil and salt and pepper. Press the tomato and pepper juices through a strainer, add them to the dish and mix everything gently. Bake in an oven preheated to the highest possible temperature for about 20 minutes. Let cool and serve.

Ingredients
2 large red peppers
2 large ripe tomatoes
3 tbsp olive oil
2 garlic cloves, finely chopped
1 tbsp chopped fresh marjoram
salt and freshly ground black pepper

Serves 4 as a tapa

Piperada
Basque-style eggs

*P*iperada is a filling egg dish, which makes a delicious brunch and it can also be served as a tapa. A popular variation of this recipe serves the piperada on toasted bread rounds dripping with butter. Either way, this simple egg dish is sure to become a part of your culinary repertoire.

Heat the oil in a frying pan and sauté the onions, peppers and garlic until tender. Fold in the ham and tomatoes and season with salt and pepper. Continue to heat until the vegetables are almost cooked.

Lightly beat the eggs with a fork. Pour the eggs over the vegetables and cook over low heat until the eggs are firm but still soft. Garnish with parsley and serve warm.

Ingredients

4 tbsp olive oil

2 small onions, peeled and finely diced

1 medium green pepper, deseeded and sliced
　into thin strips

1 medium red pepper, deseeded and sliced
　into thin strips

2 cloves garlic, peeled and minced

1 slice cured ham, cut into strips

2 large tomatoes, chopped

salt and pepper, to taste

4 eggs

chopped parsley, to garnish

Serves 2 as a main course or 4 as a tapa

Esparragos con dos salsas
White asparagus with two sauces

W hite asparagus is highly regarded in Spain. It is grown in Navarre and transported from there across the whole of Spain. You can use tinned asparagus if you cannot obtain the fresh spears.

Drain the asparagus well and put it on a dish. For the vinaigrette, mix oil, vinegar, salt and pepper together in a jug. For the tomato sauce, chop the tomato flesh into neat dice. Mix in the onion and parsley and season lightly with salt and either paprika or cayenne pepper.

To serve, arrange the tomato sauce in neat piles round the asparagus. Hand the vinaigrette round separately and allow everyone to pour their own. Eat the asparagus with one sauce, then the other.

Ingredients
400 g (14 oz) asparagus, freshly cooked
100 ml (4 fl. oz) olive oil
3 tbsp wine vinegar
salt and freshly ground black pepper
2 ripe tomatoes, skinned and deseeded
1 tbsp chopped onion
1 tbsp chopped fresh parsley
pinch hot paprika or cayenne pepper

Serves 4 as a tapa

Berenjenas rellenas de hongros

Mushroom-stuffed aubergines

Ingredients

2 aubergines
2 small onions, chopped
2 tbsp olive oil
3 garlic cloves, finely chopped
200 g (7 oz) mushrooms, cleaned and sliced
salt and freshly ground black pepper
50 g (2 oz) Parmesan cheese, grated

Serves 4 as a starter

*A*ubergines were introduced to Spain by the Moors in the early Middle Ages. Since then they have been one of the peninsula's favourite vegetables.

Halve the aubergines lengthwise and remove the flesh carefully so that the skin is not broken. Reserve the skins and chop the flesh finely.

Meanwhile, fry the onions in the oil in a frying pan until they begin to colour. Add the garlic and mushrooms and cook until they soften. Add the aubergine flesh and fry until golden, stirring occasionally. Season the aubergine skins and the flesh in the pan and then stuff the skins with the fried mixture.

Arrange the stuffed vegetables in a gratin dish and sprinkle with the cheese. Brown under a hot grill for 5 minutes and serve.

Bacalao a la vizcaina
Salt cod in spicy tomato sauce

Salt cod is very popular in Mediterranean countries, where its delicate balance of salty and fishy tastes is greatly admired – as caviar is elsewhere. You must soak the fish for 24 hours, or even longer if it is stiff as a board with a greyish tinge. Take out the best pieces to use in this exquisite dish; the rest can be saved for stews and salads.

Grill the red peppers, giving them a quarter turn every 5 minutes, until they are charred on all sides. Put them in a plastic bag for 10 minutes. Then skin and halve them, discarding stalks and seeds. Cut the flesh into strips. Soak the choricero peppers, if using, for 30 minutes. Drain the salt cod, reserving 3 fl. oz of the soaking water. Put the fish in a large saucepan with the bay leaf and parsley stalks. Cover with water, bring to a boil and remove immediately from the heat. Let cool.

Remove any bones from the fish, but keep the skin. Blot the fish dry, then dust with flour and fry in the oil, heated to a high temperature, until golden. Reserve but do not try to keep the fish warm. Fry the onions in the same oil. Before they colour, add the garlic cloves and chopped tomatoes. If you have choriceros, scrape out the pulp and add it to the pan. Add the reserved fish liquid. If not using choriceros, add the tomato paste and cayenne pepper now. When the sauce looks thick, purée it in a blender. Taste for seasoning: lemon juice will make it spicier. On the other hand, if it is too spicy, clear honey will subdue it.

Pour half the tomato sauce into an ovenproof dish and arrange the pieces of fish over it. Cover with the rest of the sauce and garnish with strips of red pepper.

Ingredients
4 portions of salt cod, soaked (see page 111)
2 red bell peppers
10 choricero peppers (optional)
1 bay leaf
4 parsley stalks
1½ tbsp flour
4 tbsp olive oil
12 oz onions, peeled and sliced
3 garlic cloves
2 large ripe tomatoes, skinned and deseeded
1 tbsp tomato paste (optional)
pinch of cayenne pepper (optional)
1 tsp lemon juice (optional)
¼ tsp honey (optional)

Serves 4 as a tapa

Ensalada de bacalao
Salt cod salad

This intensely savoury salad is very appetising, combining salty flavours with a sharp dressing. A little salt cod goes a long way in this dish, as its flavour is quite strong.

Cover the fish with water and soak in a medium saucepan for 2 hours, changing the water after the first hour.

Drain the fish. Return to the saucepan with fresh water and bring to a boil, then simmer for 20 minutes. Remove the pan from the heat, drain the fish and leave until cool enough to handle.

Flake the fish, being sure to discard all the skin and dark meat. Combine the flaked fish with the onion, olives, olive oil and vinegar in a mixing bowl. Serve chilled, garnished with parsley and lemon wedges.

Ingredients

450 g (1 lb) salt cod
1 medium white onion, diced
6 jumbo green olives, pitted
  and sliced
4 tbsp olive oil
2 tbsp red wine vinegar
fresh parsley and lemon wedges, to garnish

Serves 4 as a tapa

Fritas de bacalao
Salt cod fritters

Ingredients

175 ml (6 fl. oz) milk
225 g (½ lb) salt cod, soaked for 24 hours
1 large potato, peeled, cooked and mashed
1 shallot, finely chopped
2 tbsp chopped fresh parsley
ground black pepper
juice of ½ lemon, plus 1 tsp
2 tbsp plain flour
1 egg, beaten
4 tbsp dry breadcrumbs
sunflower oil, for frying
100 ml (4 fl. oz) mayonnaise
1½ garlic cloves, crushed

Serves 4 as a tapa

Try to avoid the drier end pieces of salt cod when making this dish—the tender middle section will give a more juicy and flavourful result. Remember to drain the cod and change the soaking water several times during its 24 hours of submersion.

Bring the milk to a simmer in a medium pan. Add the cod and poach gently for about 10 minutes, until the fish flakes easily. Remove any skin and bones and flake the flesh into a bowl. Add the potatoes, shallot and parsley and mix well. Season with black pepper and add the juice of ½ lemon.

Shape the mixture into 8–12 patties, dust with flour, dip in beaten egg, then coat in breadcrumbs. Place on a platter or tray, cover and chill for at least 30 minutes.

Meanwhile, combine the mayonnaise, garlic and remaining lemon juice and add a little black pepper. Transfer to a bowl and set aside. Heat about 2.5 cm (1 inch) sunflower oil in a large pan. Add the patties in batches and fry for about 3 minutes on each side, until golden. Drain on paper towels and serve with the garlic mayonnaise.

Biscay Bay sole with cream and shellfish

Lenguada a la vizcaina

Ingredients

2 tbsp chopped onion
6 black peppercorns
4 tbsp chopped fresh parsley
1 bay leaf
7 fl. oz dry white wine
16 clams or mussels, cleaned
4 tbsp butter
4 sole fillets
1½ tbsp flour
salt and freshly ground pepper
4 fl. oz whipping cream

Serves 4

*S*ole are fished throughout the Bay of Biscay, as far down as the Basque coast. This type of old-fashioned cooking, with a rich sauce, has been popular for over a century. Shellfish make the perfect garnish and cooked in this way they provide the stock for the dish.

Put the chopped onion in a saucepan with the peppercorns, 2 tablespoons of parsley, the bay leaf and the wine. Bring to a simmer. Put in the clams or mussels, cover and cook for 1–2 minutes until they open. Remove the shellfish, then let the liquid boil for 5 minutes and reserve. Take one shell off each mussel (discarding any that are still shut).

Melt the butter in a frying pan. Dust the fish fillets in a seasoned flour and fry, 2 at a time, for a couple of minutes on each side. Transfer to a warm plate and keep warm.

Add 1 teaspoon of flour to the pan and stir in the butter. Strain in the reserved shellfish stock, add the cream and stir to deglaze the pan. Boil to reduce the sauce by half, adding the shellfish to warm them. This sauce should need no seasoning, but taste to check. Pour it over the sole, sprinkle with parsley and serve. Slim roasted leeks make a good accompaniment to this dish.

Sunset on San Juan de Gaztelugatxe, an island off the Bay of Biscay.

Patatas con sepias y almejas
Potatoes with cuttlefish, clams and peppers

This is a simple dish of potatoes in a green sauce, with a fresh sea flavour coming from the two kinds of shellfish. Cuttlefish are well suited to stewing as their tough flesh is softened by the long, slow cooking. Substitute a large squid if cuttlefish are unavailable.

Cut the tentacles off the cuttlefish or squid and separate them. Cut the body into thick strips. Put 2 tablespoons of oil in a large saucepan and fry the garlic cloves until they colour. Transfer to a mortar.

Add 2 more tablespoons of oil and fry the onion and ham over medium heat. When the onion starts to colour, add the cuttlefish or squid and cook until the strips stiffen. Add the peppers and stir for a couple of minutes. Add the potatoes, along with 600 ml (1 pint) of water to barely cover. Season with salt and bring to a simmer.

Mash the garlic to a paste in the mortar, working in 2 tablespoons of parsley, the saffron and the wine. Stir this, with some pepper, into the casserole. Cook until the potatoes are almost tender (about 20 minutes). Remove the lid halfway through, to evaporate some of the liquid.

Add the clams and simmer for 2 more minutes. Check the seasonings and sprinkle with the remaining parsley.

Ingredients

450 g (1 lb) cuttlefish or squid, cleaned
4 tbsp olive oil
2 garlic cloves
1 onion, chopped
50 g (2 oz) raw ham, diced
2 green peppers, deseeded and cut into strips
900 g (2 lb) potatoes, peeled and diced
salt and freshly ground black pepper
6 tbsp chopped fresh parsley
5 saffron strands
4 tbsp white wine
450 g (1 lb) clams, cleaned

Serves 4 as a main course or 6 as a tapa

Cuttlefish, clams and other seafood on sale in a typically well-stocked Spanish fish market.

Chilindrón de cordero
Lamb and roasted pepper stew

*P*iquillo peppers are roasted and tinned Spanish sweet peppers.
If you can't find them, substitute any roasted peppers.

Coat the bottom of a large saucepan with olive oil and heat. Add the lamb and brown on all sides. Remove the lamb from the pan and add the onions, garlic and ham. Cook until the vegetables become soft.

Add the piquillo peppers; deglaze the pan by adding the sherry, port and white wine. Bring to a boil then reduce the heat and simmer until the mixture is reduced by half.

Return the lamb to the pan and add the tomatoes, bay leaf and rosemary. Simmer for 3 hours. Serve with boiled rice and red beans.

Ingredients

olive oil, for cooking
1.5 kg (3 lb) lamb shoulder
1 onion, peeled and chopped
4 garlic cloves, finely chopped
100 g (4 oz) Serrano ham, sliced
100 g (4 oz) drained piquillo peppers
200 ml (7 fl. oz) dry (fino) or semi-dry
   (amontillado) sherry
200 ml (7 fl. oz) ruby port
200 ml (7 fl. oz) dry white wine
275 g (10 oz) tinned whole tomatoes
1 bay leaf
2 sprigs fresh rosemary
boiled rice and red beans, to serve

Serves 4 as a main course

Alubias de Tolosa
Tolosa red bean stew with pork

*T*olosa, *in the Basque Country, is famous for its kidney beans, which are long and as black as coal. Basques adore red beans, too, so use whichever red beans are available to you. This traditional dish contains the red chorizo sausage and the black morcilla, along with cured pork. This recipe can work equally well as a starter or tapa for 6.*

Drain the beans and put them in a saucepan with the pork and half the chopped onion. Add 1 tablespoon of oil and cover with water. Bring to the boil, then turn down the heat, cover the pan and simmer gently for 2 hours or until the meat is tender. Take care that the water level remains high enough to cover the stew, adding more water in small quantities if necessary.

Heat the rest of the oil in a frying pan. Slice and fry the chorizos and morcillo or black pudding with the chopped pepper.

Remove the pork or bacon from the pan and chop it into cubes. Check the amount of liquid remaining in the pan: it should now be well reduced. If not, discard some. Return the meat to the pan and season everything well.

Fry the remaining onion in the same pan used for the sausage, adding the garlic at the end. Stir into the beans and simmer for a further 10 minutes.

Ingredients
450 g (1 lb) red beans, soaked overnight
150 g (5 oz) pork belly or boiling bacon, in
  one piece
1 large onion, finely chopped
4 tbsp olive oil
2 chorizo sausages
1 morcillo or 150 g (5 oz) black pudding
1 large green pepper, deseeded and chopped
salt and freshly ground black pepper
2 garlic cloves, finely chopped

Serves 4 as a main course

Flan de naranjas
Orange flan

Although meals in Spain usually end with a piece of fresh fruit, Spaniards eagerly consume prepared desserts on special occasions or holidays. Flan, in particular, tops the list of Spanish dessert favourites. While most flans resemble traditional custard desserts, this flan is infused with a delicate orange flavour, a lingering reminder of Spain's Moorish past.

Preheat the oven to 180°C (350°F). To make the caramel topping, heat the sugar and the water in a small saucepan, swirling gently until a golden brown caramel is formed. Immediately divide the mixture evenly among four individual ramekins. Swirl and tilt the ramekins to ensure that the caramel coats the ramekins' sides and bases. Place the ramekins in a baking pan.

In a small bowl, bring the orange juice and orange rind to a boil, then remove from the heat. Meanwhile, in a separate bowl, whisk together the eggs and egg yolks with the remaining sugar, until the mixture is thick. Pour in the orange juice and rind, stirring constantly.

Divide this mixture among the four ramekins in the baking pan, then pour boiling water around them to create a bain-marie. Bake in the oven for about 25 minutes or until lightly set. Allow to cool, then refrigerate overnight.

Immediately before serving, briefly immerse the bases of the ramekins in hot water and, if necessary, pass a knife around the outer edges of the ramekins to make unmoulding easier. Invert and unmould the desserts onto serving saucers. Decorate with fresh orange slices or candied orange peel.

Ingredients

150 g (5 oz) sugar, for the caramel topping
120 ml (4 fl. oz) water, for the caramel topping
450 ml (15 fl. oz) freshly squeezed orange juice
grated rind of 1 orange
4 medium eggs, plus 2 medium egg yolks
150 g (5 oz) sugar
fresh orange slices or candied orange peel, to decorate

Serves 4

Intxaursalsa
Festive walnut cream

Ingredients
500 ml (18 fl. oz) milk
110 g (4½ oz) sugar
strip of lemon zest
½ cinnamon stick
110 g (4½ oz) shelled walnuts
1 slice stale bread, crusts removed and lightly
   toasted
100 ml (3½ fl. oz) single cream
ground cinnamon

Serves 4

*T*his chilled walnut cream is served as a dessert on festive occasions, especially Christmas Eve.

Bring the milk to a boil with the sugar, lemon zest and cinnamon stick. Reduce the heat. Grind the walnuts in a food processor, being careful not to over-grind or they will turn oily. Add the ground nuts to the milk and simmer for 30 minutes.

Rub the bread into crumbs and add it to the pan. Simmer briefly, then remove the zest and cinnamon. Off the heat, beat with a wooden spoon or purée in a food processor. Stir in the cream, return to the heat and simmer gently for 2–3 more minutes.

Chill well and serve very cold, lightly dusted with cinnamon.

CHAPTER 4

Catalonia

GIRONA ⊙

Catalonia

BARCELONA ⊙

TARRAGONA ⊙

Catalonia, in the north-eastern corner of Spain, is home to some 7 million people who consider themselves to be a people apart from the rest of the country. They are recognized as being largely autonomous and their culture and language are quite distinct. Catalonia today is a dynamic region whose capital Barcelona, in particular, is proud of its individual character. Just as distinctive is the regional cuisine, based around simple staples such as toasted bread, rubbed with olive oil and spread with tomatoes. Understandably in a coastal region, the fish and shellfish are excellent. Meat is often combined with seafood in a style of cooking called mar i muntanya – the sea and the mountains.

La Boqueria market, with its vast array of produce, has been at the center of Barcelona's shopping culture since it opened in the nineteenth century. There has been a market on this site, just off La Rambla, for 800 years.

Escalivada
Roasted vegetable salad

*F*rom the Catalan verb escalivar, meaning 'to cook over hot
embers', escalivada is a colourful array of vegetables, roasted to
perfection and glistening with olive oil. Escalivada is usually served
on a rustic, earthenware platter and, as with most tapas, should be
accompanied by thick slices of fresh crusty bread.

Lay the onions on a baking sheet and bake in the oven at 180°C (350°F) for 10 minutes. Add the aubergine and bake for a further 10 minutes. Add the peppers, tomatoes and half of the garlic cloves and bake until all vegetables are tender. Remove the vegetables from the oven and allow to cool.

Peel the vegetables with your fingers. Cut the aubergine into strips. Remove the stem, core and seeds from the bell peppers and cut into strips as well. Deeed the tomatoes, then slice into wedges. Thinly slice the onion. Arrange the vegetables attractively on a serving platter.

In a food processor, combine the roasted garlic, the remaining cloves of raw garlic, the cumin seeds, lemon juice, vinegar, olive oil, sweet paprika and rosemary. When the mixture is smooth and homogenized, pour it evenly over the vegetables. Season with salt and serve.

Ingredients

2 medium yellow onions, unpeeled
1 medium aubergine
1 large green pepper
1 large red pepper
1 large yellow pepper
2 medium tomatoes
8 cloves garlic
2 tsp cumin seeds
2 tbsp lemon juice
3 tbsp sherry vinegar
4 tbsp olive oil
1 tsp sweet paprika
1 tsp chopped fresh rosemary
salt, to taste

Serves 4 as a tapa

Xató

Frisée salad with cured fish

Ingredients

90 g (3½ oz) soaked salt cod

1 head frisée or escarole

50-g (2-oz) tin anchovies, drained

1 tbsp olive oil

1 tbsp sherry vinegar

4 tbsp romesco sauce (see page 138)

100-g (4-oz) tin tuna, drained and flaked

2 handfuls small green olives

Serves 6 as a tapa

*S*pain produces a bigger range of cured fish than any other
country in the Mediterranean. Here three of the common ones
are combined with crisp green leaves and a sophisticated dressing
of hazelnuts and chillies. The dish is pronounced the way 'château'
is said in English. The cod must be free of all skin and bones and
soaked to the point where it is not completely desalinated – so it is
poised at the appetising point between being salted and fresh.

Separate the frisée or escarole leaves, wash them, dry well and chill. Drain the cod and pat dry with paper towel. Pull the flesh apart into flakes and small strips. Cut the anchovy fillets into small pieces on the diagonal.

Put the frisée in a big, shallow salad bowl. Stir the oil and sherry vinegar into the romesco sauce and check the seasonings – it should be distinctly piquant. Spoon the sauce over the salad and toss until it is well distributed.

Add the salt cod and the tuna, separated into its natural flakes and toss again. Serve on individual plates, distributing the anchovy fillets and olives evenly over the leaves.

Espinacas Catalanas
Catalan-style spinach with raisins and pine nuts

*S*weet, plump raisins and crisp pine nuts are often paired together *in classic Catalan cuisine. Try them tossed with fresh spinach and stuffed olives. This traditional combination is excellent as a tapa or as a side dish. As a variation, omit the croûtons and serve the spinach on toasted bread slices.*

Heat the olive oil in a frying pan. Add the garlic and onion and fry gently until golden. Set aside.

Rinse the spinach and trim the leaves from the stalks. Discard the stalks. Place the spinach in a large saucepan, cover and cook over low heat for 10 minutes in the water clinging to its leaves. Drain, then stir the spinach into the onion and garlic. Mix in the raisins, pine nuts and olives. Season generously with salt and pepper. Transfer to a serving dish, sprinkle croûtons on top and serve warm.

Ingredients

3 tbsp olive oil
2 cloves garlic, finely chopped
1 medium onion, finely chopped
900 g (2 lb) spinach
65 g (2½ oz) raisins, soaked in hot water for
   20 minutes and drained
4 tbsp pine nuts
50 g (2 oz) pimento-stuffed olives,
   finely chopped
salt and pepper, to taste
croûtons, to serve

Serves 4–6 as a tapa

Paella esmeralda
Emerald paella

*B*ased on Catalonia's spinach with raisins and pine nuts (page 130), this vegetable paella owes its name to the generous use of green peppers, parsley, olives and spinach that flavour the rice. The dish can include raisins too, if you like. Although not a traditional accompaniment to paella, they can add an unexpected and welcome sweetness to the saffron-enhanced rice.

Combine the vegetable stock, parsley, basil, saffron and cumin in a saucepan and heat over low heat. Set aside.

Heat the olive oil in the paella pan and lightly toast the pine nuts. Add the onion, garlic and pepper and sauté until tender. Add the olives and the spinach and cook for several minutes, until the spinach has wilted.

Mix in the rice and pour in the warm vegetable stock, combining well. Cook until the rice is tender and all the stock has been absorbed, about 25 minutes. Mix in the cheese and allow to cool for several minutes before serving.

Ingredients

900 ml (1½ pints) vegetable stock
1½ tbsp chopped fresh parsley
1 tsp dried basil
½ tsp saffron
¼ tsp ground cumin
75 ml (3 fl. oz) olive oil
4 tbsp pine nuts
1 large onion, finely chopped
8 cloves garlic, finely chopped
1 medium green pepper, finely chopped
175 g (6 oz) pimento-stuffed olives, chopped
275 g (10 oz) spinach leaves, destemmed and chopped
325 g (12 oz) paella rice
40 g (1½ oz) grated Manchego or Parmesan cheese

Serves 6 as a main course, 8–10 as a tapa

Paella de rape a la Catalana
Catalan-style paella with monkfish

This paella features monkfish, which has gained in popularity in recent years. Prepared and cooked correctly, monkfish looks and tastes much like lobster. Here, the subtle flavour and tenderness of the monkfish add the perfect accents to the plump, juicy rice. A chilled white wine is an ideal accompaniment to this seafood paella.

Heat 175 ml (6 fl. oz) of the olive oil in a paella pan over medium to high heat. Lightly fry the monkfish pieces all over and transfer to a platter.

In the same oil, sauté the chilli and transfer to a mortar. Fry the slice of bread in the same oil until golden and transfer to the mortar with the chilli. Mash together until a paste is formed.

Add the chopped garlic and tomatoes to the paella pan and sauté for several minutes. Pour in the remaining oil and, when sufficiently heated, add the rice. Place the monkfish pieces on top and add the stock, mashed chilli and bread and the saffron. Cook for 20–25 minutes, or until the liquid has been absorbed and the rice is tender.

Season with salt and pepper and serve immediately.

Ingredients
225 ml (8 fl. oz) olive oil
700 g (1½ lb) monkfish, cut into pieces
1 small fresh chilli pepper
1 slice white bread
5 cloves garlic, finely chopped
2 medium tomatoes, skinned, deseeded and
    chopped
450 g (1 lb) paella rice
1 litre (2 pints) fish or chicken stock
¼ tsp saffron
salt and pepper, to taste

Serves 6 as a main course, 8–10 as a tapa

Zarzuela
Fish stew

*T*he name zarzuela – literally a light, whimsical operetta – perfectly reflects the bright colours and vibrancy of this unforgettable feast of fish. This dish should be served with fresh crusty bread to mop up the delicious juices.

Heat the oil in a large pan and cook the onion and garlic until tender. Add the tomatoes, bay leaf, oregano and saffron. Cook for about 10 minutes, stirring occasionally. Increase the heat to high and add the monkfish, clam juice, wine and parsley. Bring to a boil, then add the clams, mussels, prawns and squid. Reduce the heat to medium, cover and cook for about a further 10 minutes.

Discard any mussels and clams that have failed to open. Remove and discard the bay leaf. Season with salt and pepper, transfer to an earthenware serving bowl and garnish with chopped parsley. Serve immediately, with crusty bread.

Ingredients

100 ml (4 fl. oz) olive oil

1 medium onion, peeled and chopped

2 cloves garlic, finely chopped

2 medium tomatoes, skinned, deseeded and diced

1 bay leaf

¼ tsp oregano

¼ tsp saffron

225 g (8 oz) monkfish, skinned and cut into chunks

450 ml (16 fl. oz) clam juice

100 ml (4 fl. oz) dry white wine

1 tbsp chopped parsley

12 clams, scrubbed

12 mussels, scrubbed and debearded

225 g (8 oz) prawns, peeled and deveined

225 g (8 oz) squid, cleaned and sliced into rings

salt and pepper, to taste

chopped parsley, to garnish

crusty bread, to serve

Serves 4 as a main course

Langosta a la Catalana
Catalan-style lobster

Ingredients

100 g (4 oz) finely sliced Serrano or Parma
    ham
2 tinned red pimientos, drained
4 tbsp Spanish olive oil
1 medium onion, finely chopped
2 cloves garlic, finely chopped
325 g (12 oz) tinned chopped tomatoes
100 ml (4 fl. oz) dry white wine
4 small cooked lobsters
4 tbsp brandy
salt and freshly ground black pepper
2 tbsp chopped fresh parsley
chopped fresh parsley and lemon wedges,
    to garnish

Serves 4 as a main course, 8 as a tapa

If lobster is too expensive, this dish works just as well with large prawns. Rich and delicious, this lobster goes well with a crisp salad and rice, or some bread, to mop up the sauce.

Cut the ham and pimientos into thin strips. Heat the olive oil in a frying pan and gently fry the onion and garlic for 5 minutes until softened. Add the ham and cook, stirring, for a further 2 minutes.

Add the pimientos, tomatoes and wine, bring to a boil and simmer, uncovered, for 15 minutes or until thickened.

Meanwhile, wash and pat dry the lobsters and cut in half lengthwise. Add the lobsters to the sauce, making sure they are completely submerged. Add the brandy, seasoning and parsley and heat through gently for 4–5 minutes.

Pile on to warm serving plates, garnish with some parsley and serve with the wedges of lemon to squeeze over.

Pescado con salsa romesco
Flat fish with hazelnut and chilli sauce

Small flat fish, simply fried, are a flavourful treat – especially when moist and slightly underdone. The sauce, salsa romesco, is a famous and sophisticated Catalan favourite.

Start the sauce by toasting the nuts in a low oven (150°C/300°F) for 20 minutes until biscuit-coloured. Fry the garlic, then the bread slice, in 4 tablespoons olive oil and reserve. Add the chopped tomato and chilli or cayenne pepper to the pan and cook, stirring, until the mixture has thickened. Season with salt and pepper.

Grind the nuts in a blender. Add the bread, garlic, vinegar and fino sherry and pulverise everything. Stir this into the tomato sauce. Check the seasoning.

Dust the sole with seasoned flour. Heat the butter and oil in a frying pan. When very hot, put in the fish. Whole fish need 3–4 minutes for the first side, 2 minutes for the second. If using fillets, allow about 2 minutes each side.

Serve on hot plates and pass the sauce round in a bowl.

Ingredients

25 g (1 oz) blanched hazelnuts
2 garlic cloves, finely chopped
4–6 tbsp olive oil
1 slice stale bread
1 large ripe tomato, skinned and deseeded
½ dried chilli or a pinch of cayenne pepper
salt and freshly ground black pepper
2 tsp red wine vinegar
4 tbsp fino sherry
4 small lemon sole or other flatfish, cleaned
2 tbsp flour
salt and pepper
2 tbsp butter
1 tbsp olive oil

Serves 4 as a main course

Costa Brava shoreline near Lloret de Mar, Catalonia.

Porc amb musclos
Pork with mussels

Ingredients

775 g (1¾ lb) lean pork, cubed
salt and freshly ground black pepper
2 tbsp lard
2 tbsp olive oil
700 g (1½ lb) onions, chopped
6 garlic cloves, finely chopped
325-g (12-oz) tin tomatoes
1 tbsp paprika
½ dried chilli, deseeded and chopped
2 bay leaves
1 strip dried or 2 strips fresh orange peel
1.5 kg (3 lb) mussels, cleaned
200 ml (7 fl. oz) dry white wine
6 tbsp chopped fresh parsley

Serves 8 as a main course or 12 as a tapa

So-called 'sea and mountain' dishes like this one were originally an economical way of eking out small quantities. Later they became more lavish, with combinations like chicken and lobster.

Heat the lard in a wide saucepan. Season the pork well and fry in the melted lard until it is golden on all sides. Remove from the pan. Add the oil and chopped onions and cook gently until soft. Add the garlic, tomatoes (breaking them up with a spoon), paprika, chilli, bay leaves and orange peel. Cook for 20 minutes until reduced.

Meanwhile put the mussels in a big saucepan over medium heat until they open, then remove. Put in the wine and 2 tablespoons of parsley. Add half the shellfish and cover tightly. Steam for 4 minutes, shaking the pan occasionally if they are not all in one layer. Remove the first batch of mussels from the pan and cook the second batch. Remove the top shells from each mussel and throw away any mussels that smell strongly or remain shut.

Add the pork and the mussel liquor to the sauce and simmer for 30 minutes, until the meat is tender and the sauce is reduced. Check the seasoning, add the mussels and warm through. Sprinkle with parsley and serve.

A wide range of pork products are enjoyed across Spain. A distinctively Catalonian touch is to combine them with seafood.

Crema Catalana
Sweet Catalan cream

Because of its crisp, caramelized topping, this creamy Catalan dessert is often compared to the French crème brûlée. Sweet Catalan cream, however, is not as heavy or rich as its French cousin and thus makes a more pleasant ending to a heavy dinner.

In a saucepan, bring the milk, cinnamon stick, lemon rind and vanilla extract to a boil. Simmer for several minutes, then discard the cinnamon stick and lemon rind. Set the flavoured milk aside.

In a bowl, whisk the egg yolks together with the cornflour and 150 g (5 ounces) of the sugar until the mixture is creamy. Gradually pour this mixture into the saucepan with the milk, mixing continuously.

Slowly heat the mixture until it begins to thicken, taking care that it does not boil. Pour into four ramekins or heatproof cups, allow to cool and refrigerate for several hours.

Immediately before serving, preheat the grill and sprinkle the remaining sugar evenly over each serving. Place the dishes under the grill until the sugar topping begins to caramelize. Remove from the grill and serve.

Ingredients
450 ml (15 fl. oz) milk
1 cinnamon stick
rind of 1 lemon
1 tsp vanilla extract
4 medium egg yolks
1 tbsp cornflour
200 g (7 oz) caster sugar

Serves 4

CHAPTER 5

Eastern Spain

T he east of Spain is perhaps most famous for its fine beaches, especially the tourist-oriented coasts of the Balearic Islands. But the cuisine of these provinces also earns them renown; Valencia is known worldwide for its oranges and its rice fields. Paella was created here two centuries ago and there are now scores of versions as well as many other rice dishes. The east coast also has Alicante, with its date palms and African climate and Murcia, which remained under Arab rule until the seventeenth century.

The fort of Dénia overlooking this small coastal town in Alicante province.

Tumbet
Aubergine casserole

*T*umbet, the traditional aubergine dish of the Balearic Islands, can stand on its own as a main course, or can be served as an accompaniment to heartier meat dishes. While many chefs choose to serve tumbet fresh from the oven, this dish is also delectable when left to cool and eaten at room temperature.

Leave the aubergine slices in a colander for 1 hour. Blot with paper towels.

Heat the olive oil in a frying pan over low heat. Fry the potato slices until golden, then arrange them on the bottom of a heatproof casserole dish and season with salt and pepper. In the same oil, lightly fry the aubergine slices. Transfer to the dish and layer the aubergine on top of the potato. Fry the peppers in the same oil, transfer to the casserole and arrange them on top of the aubergine. Fry the courgettes in the same oil, transfer to the casserole dish and layer over the peppers. Season again.

Fry the minced garlic in the same frying pan, adding more oil if necessary, until golden. Mix in the chopped tomatoes and cook over medium heat for about 20 minutes.

Pass the tomato sauce through a sieve, sprinkle with sugar and pour over the vegetables in the casserole. Transfer to a 350°F (180°C) oven and bake for about 10 minutes. The aubergine casserole can be served hot or at room temperature.

Ingredients

3 medium aubergines, cut into 5-mm (¼-inch) slices and sprinkled with salt
225 ml (8 fl. oz) olive oil
2 large potatoes, sliced thin
salt and pepper, to taste
2 small red peppers, chopped
3 small courgettes, sliced
3 cloves garlic, minced
2 large tomatoes, skinned, deseeded and chopped
pinch of sugar

Serves 4 as a main course, 8 as a tapa

Bajoques farcides
Baked peppers with rice stuffing

Ingredients

3 tbsp olive oil

1 large chicken breast, diced

150 g (5 oz) lean pork, diced

100 g (4 oz) ham or smoked bacon, diced

200 g (7 oz) short-grain rice

2 garlic cloves, finely chopped

900 g (2 lb) ripe tomatoes, skinned, deseeded and chopped

1 green pepper, finely chopped

3 tbsp sweetcorn

2 tsp paprika

pinch powdered saffron

salt and freshly ground black pepper

6 tbsp chopped fresh parsley

6 large red peppers

Serves 6 as a light main course

*T*he title of this recipe is the Valencian dialect name for rice-stuffed peppers. This delicate version comes from Alcoy.

Heat the oil in a large saucepan and fry the chicken, pork and ham or bacon until coloured on all sides. Remove from the heat and reserve.

Meanwhile, cook the rice in plenty of boiling salted water until done – this usually takes about 15 minutes, but follow the instructions on the packet. Drain and reserve the rice.

Add the garlic, chopped tomatoes, green pepper, sweetcorn, paprika, saffron, salt and pepper and parsley to the pan containing the meat. Let the sauce simmer to reduce the volume of liquid by about half. Stir the rice into the sauce.

Oil a deep ovenproof dish big enough to take all the peppers. Cut off 'lids' at the stalk ends of the peppers and remove the seeds. Stuff them with the meat and rice mixture and replace the lids. Tuck the peppers into the dish, cover with foil and bake at 170°C (325°F) for 1¼ hours.

Zarangollo
Courgette and onion hash

This is a very traditional dish, still eaten in the same way as it was before the introduction of American vegetables to Spain. After Columbus's voyage, peppers and tomatoes were added to this base to make pisto and ratatouille. The onions are softened in oil, then the vegetables cook in their own juices. Sometimes, to make the dish more substantial, eggs are scrambled in.

Put the oil in a heavy-based saucepan and add the onion. Cook very slowly for about 10 minutes, adding the garlic as the onion begins to soften. Add the courgettes and season with salt and pepper. Stir gently for a couple of minutes. Cover with foil and the saucepan lid and cook over low heat for 30 minutes.

Stir, breaking up the courgettes with a wooden spoon. Add the oregano, re-cover the pot and cook slowly for another 30 minutes, until everything is soft and amalgamated. Remove the lid for the last 10 minutes, to allow some of the juices to evaporate.

Serve with fried bread.

Ingredients
50 ml (2 fl. oz) olive oil
1 onion, peeled and finely sliced
2 garlic cloves, finely chopped
900 g (2 lb) courgettes, peeled and
  finely sliced
salt and freshly ground black pepper
½ tbsp chopped fresh oregano
fried bread, to serve

Serves 2 as a main course, 4 as a tapa

Ensalada Murciana
Murcian salad of mixed baked vegetables

Ingredients

550 g (1 lb 4 oz) aubergine

3 green peppers

4 medium onions, peeled

4 large tomatoes

1 bunch spring onions, trimmed

8 tbsp olive oil

3 garlic cloves, bruised

juice of 1 lemon

salt and freshly ground black pepper

4 tbsp chopped fresh parsley

Serves 4 as a main course

*L*ike the Catalan escalivada (page 126), the vegetables used to make this salad are baked round the edge of the barbecue in summer, then dressed to serve cold. Here they are baked in the oven and make a good vegetarian main course. You could alter the selection of vegetables – just modify cooking times to suit them.

Preheat the oven to 200°C (400°F). Put the aubergine, peppers, onions, tomatoes and spring onions into a large ovenproof dish with the oil and garlic cloves. Also add 5 tablespoons cold water to stop the juices burning. Bake the vegetables for 25 minutes, then remove the tomatoes. After another 15 minutes, remove the peppers. Give the other vegetables a squeeze to see how close they are to being done. Put the peppers in a plastic bag; this helps with the skinning later. The aubergine will probably be ready in about another 15 minutes, but onions usually need another 15 minutes or more. Stir the juices in the dish and pour them into a cup, discarding the garlic cloves.

Skin the tomatoes and arrange them in the centre of a big platter, then just cut them across like a star. Skin the rest of the vegetables, slice them lengthways and keep all the juices they exude. Arrange the vegetables in sets on the platter, radiating round the tomatoes. Sprinkle lemon juice over the salad and season. Then stir the reserved pan juices and dribble some into the centre of the tomatoes and over the salad. Sprinkle with parsley and serve.

Palm trees and waterfall in Elche Murcia, Spain.

Paella mixta
Seafood, sausage and chicken paella

*T*his is the recipe that springs to mind when most people think of paella. While Valencia, the homeland of paella, rarely cooks it using a mixture of seafood with meat, this version has caught the popular imagination outside Spain and tends to be the one served in most Spanish-themed restaurants. It is easy to understand why few could resist the combination of delicate lobster meat, mussels, clams and prawns teamed with rich chorizo sausage and tender chicken.

Scrub and debeard the mussels and clams, discarding any that do not close when tapped sharply. Set aside.

Heat 50 ml (2 fl. oz) of the olive oil in a frying pan. Add the pork and brown on all sides. Mix in the garlic, onions, tomato and peppers, stirring constantly until cooked. Remove from the pan and set aside.

In the same frying pan, heat a further 50 ml (2 fl. oz) olive oil and cook the chicken until browned on all sides. Season with salt, pepper, paprika, rosemary, thyme and cumin. Transfer the chicken to a plate and set aside. In the same frying pan, cook the lobster claws over high heat for several minutes until the shells turn pink. Transfer to a plate and set aside.

Preheat the oven to 200°C (400°F). Heat 4 tablespoons olive oil in the frying pan and sauté the rice until it is translucent. Pour in the chicken stock and combine well. Add the pork mixture, stirring constantly. Sprinkle in the saffron and continue to stir until well mixed. Transfer the rice into a paella pan. Mix in the lobster, chicken, sausage, clams, mussels, prawns, peas and capers, combining well. Bake the paella, uncovered and on the lowest oven shelf, for around 25 minutes, or until all the liquid has been absorbed.

Discard any mussels and clams that have failed to open. Serve the paella straight from the pan, garnished with lemon wedges.

Ingredients

- 10 mussels
- 10 clams
- 100 ml (4 fl. oz), plus 4 tbsp, olive oil
- 50 g (2 oz) boneless pork, diced
- 2 tsp minced garlic
- 175 g (6 oz) onions, chopped fine
- 1 medium tomato, skinned, deseeded and chopped
- 1 small red pepper, deseeded and cut into thin strips
- 1 small green pepper, deseeded and cut into thin strips
- 1 small yellow pepper, deseeded and cut into thin strips
- 900 g (2 lb) skinless, boneless chicken breasts, cut into chunks
- salt and pepper, to taste
- 1 tsp paprika
- ½ tsp dried rosemary
- ½ tsp dried thyme
- ¼ tsp ground cumin
- 700 g (1½ lb) lobster claws
- 700 g (1½ lb) paella rice
- 1 litre (2 pints) chicken stock
- ¼ tsp saffron
- 2 chorizo sausages, cooked and cut into chunks
- 10 uncooked prawns, peeled and deveined
- 100 g (4 oz) peas
- 4 tbsp capers
- lemon wedges, to garnish

Serves 6 as a main course, 8–10 as a tapa

Paella de pollo, calabacines y romero
Paella with chicken, courgettes and rosemary

Ingredients

175 ml (6 fl. oz) olive oil

1.4 kg (3 lb) chicken breasts, boned and
cut into pieces

1 large onion, chopped

5 cloves garlic, minced

1 large green pepper, chopped

75 ml (3 fl. oz) dry sherry

325 g (12 oz) paella rice

650 ml (1¼ pints) chicken stock

¼ tsp saffron

¼ tsp turmeric

3 tbsp chopped fresh rosemary

3 large courgettes, cut into 4-cm
(1½-inch) strips

salt and freshly ground black pepper

Serves 6 as a main course, 8–10 as a tapa

*T*his deliciously flavoured rice dish features tender chicken breasts subtly seasoned with fresh rosemary. It could be said that this paella brings good fortune to those who eat it, for, according to an ancient Spanish superstition, anyone who passes a rosemary bush must pull some sprigs off the fragrant shrub and pocket them to ensure good luck in the week to come.

Heat 50 ml (2 fl. oz) of the oil in a paella pan. Add the chicken and cook until done and browned on all sides. Set aside.

Clean the pan and heat the remaining olive oil over medium heat. Add the onion and cook for 5 minutes. Add the garlic and green pepper and cook for 3 minutes. Add the sherry and cook for a further minute. Pour in the rice and sauté for 5 minutes. Mix in the stock, saffron, turmeric, browned chicken and 1½ tablespoons of the rosemary and cook for 15 minutes.

Sprinkle in the remaining rosemary and stir. Arrange the courgettes over the rice, cover and cook for a further 10 minutes or until the rice and chicken are tender and the stock has been absorbed. Allow to cool for 5 minutes and serve.

Paella de gambas con Jerez
Prawn paella with sherry

The use of sherry in this dish evokes the taste of a paella served outdoors in a seaside restaurant. If you wish, lay lemon wedges around the edge of the rice for an even more attractive presentation.

Heat the oil in a paella pan over medium heat. Add the onions and garlic and sauté for about 5 minutes, or until the onion is soft. Add the peppers and cook for a further 5 minutes. Add the tomatoes and continue to cook for a further 8–10 minutes.

Add the rice and cook, stirring, for a further 5 minutes. Mix in the stock, sherry, prawns, saffron and salt and pepper. Bring to a simmer and cook gently for 20 minutes.

Boil the sliced carrots in salted water until almost tender. About 2 minutes before they are ready, add the spring onions and sugar snap peas and blanch briefly. Drain.

Arrange the carrots, spring onions and sugar snap peas on top of the rice and continue cooking until all liquid has been absorbed and the rice is tender, about 5 minutes.

Ingredients

50 ml (2 fl. oz) olive oil

2 medium onions, chopped

5 cloves garlic, minced

1 small green pepper, diced

1 small red pepper, diced

3 large tomatoes, skinned, deseeded and chopped

325 g (12 oz) paella rice

600 ml (1 pint) fish stock

225 ml (8 fl. oz) sherry

12 oz medium prawns, peeled and deveined

½ tsp saffron

salt and pepper, to taste

3 medium carrots, peeled and sliced lengthwise

6 spring onions, trimmed

3 oz sugar snap peas, halved lengthwise

Serves 6 as a main course, 8–10 as a tapa

Paella vegetariana
Vegetarian paella

Ingredients

50 ml (2 fl. oz) olive oil
1 large yellow onion, chopped
5 cloves garlic, minced
1 litre (2 pints) vegetable stock
450 g (1 lb) rice
1 small red pepper, cut into strips
1 small green pepper, cut into strips
1 small yellow pepper, cut into strips
4 medium tomatoes, deseeded and chopped
100 g (4 oz) frozen peas, defrosted
400 g (14 oz) artichoke hearts, tough outer
   leaves removed and quartered
lemon juice, to sprinkle
lemon wedges, to garnish

Serves 6 as a main course, 8–10 as a tapa

*T*his paella is so moist, full of flavour and substantial that you will scarcely notice it is meat-free. The green, red and yellow peppers add a vibrant splash of colour to the pale rice, while the tangy artichoke hearts, delicate peas and juicy tomatoes ensure that this vegetarian meal will satisfy even the most avid carnivores.

Heat the oil in a paella pan and sauté the onion and garlic until the onion is tender and translucent. At the same time, heat the stock in a separate saucepan until simmering.

Pour the rice into the paella pan and sauté for about 3 minutes. Add the peppers and tomatoes and cook for a further 3 minutes. Add the simmering vegetable stock and cook over medium heat for 20 minutes or until almost tender and almost all the liquid has been absorbed. Stir in the peas.

Sprinkle the artichoke hearts with a few drops of lemon juice and arrange over the rice in an attractive pattern. Continue cooking until the liquid has been absorbed and the rice is tender. Garnish with lemon wedges and serve.

Paella de pollo y tomates secos

Chicken paella with sun-dried tomatoes

*I*n this sophisticated paella, sun-dried tomatoes are enhanced with dry sherry and provide a flavourful contrast to the plump rice. Likewise, the interplay of mushrooms, onion and garlic lends the paella a distinct pungency that is counterbalanced by the tender chicken. The delicate balance of flavours and simple preparation make this the perfect choice for a paella supper any time.

Soak the chopped sun-dried tomatoes in the sherry for 30 minutes, then drain when ready to use.

Heat the olive oil in a paella pan over medium heat. Add the chicken and fry until browned on all sides.

Meanwhile, in a small saucepan over low heat, cook the mushrooms, onion and garlic in 3 tablespoons sherry until the mushrooms are tender. Add this mixture to the paella pan and stir well. Mix in the sun-dried tomatoes and cook for 3 minutes. Pour in the rice and cook for a further 5 minutes, stirring frequently. Add the stock, saffron and basil and cook for about 25 minutes, or until the rice and chicken are tender and the stock has been absorbed. Serve at once.

Ingredients

25 g (1 oz) sun-dried tomatoes (not packed in olive oil), chopped
175 ml (6 fl. oz) dry sherry, for soaking
100 ml (4 fl. oz) olive oil
700 g (1½ lb) skinless, boneless chicken breasts, cut into chunks
45 g (2½ oz) sliced mushrooms
½ medium onion, finely chopped
3 cloves garlic, finely chopped
3 tbsp dry sherry
325 g (12 oz) rice
900 ml (1½ pints) chicken stock
¼ tsp saffron
1 tsp dried basil

Serves 6

Paella con pasas y almendras tostadas
Paella with currants and toasted almonds

Ingredients

2 tbsp olive oil

2 medium onions, diced

4 cloves garlic, minced

325 g (12 oz) skinless, boneless chicken
breasts, cut into small chunks and seasoned
with salt and pepper

900 ml (1½ pints) chicken stock

½ tsp saffron

325 g (12 oz) paella rice

225 g (8 oz) currants

handful of fresh coriander, chopped

salt and pepper, to taste

65 g (2½ oz) slivered almonds, toasted

Serves 6 as a main course, 8–10 as a tapa

*T*his unusual recipe, combining chicken with currants and
toasted almonds, produces a crisp and succulent rice with
just a tinge of sweetness. If you do not have currants on hand, use
raisins as a substitute.

Heat the oil in a paella pan over medium heat. Add the onion and garlic and sauté until
tender. Add the chicken and cook until lightly browned on all sides, about 5 minutes.

At the same time, heat the chicken stock in a small saucepan over low heat. Add the
saffron, stir and keep over low heat until ready for use.

Add the rice to the paella pan. Pour in the stock and reduce the heat to low. Cook until
the stock has been absorbed and the rice is tender. Remove from the heat and mix in
the currants and coriander. Season with salt and pepper, sprinkle with the sliced toasted
almonds and serve.

Trempo
Balearic garden salad

*T*his pretty, fresh salad includes fruit and the local capers, which grow on the Balearic hillsides and are sold pickled to the whole of Spain.

Slice the tomatoes and peppers into rings. Line a big plate or shallow salad bowl with the tomato slices. Beat together the oil, vinegar, salt and pepper in a bowl. Peel, core and slice the pear and apple and add to the bowl at once, turning them in the dressing to prevent them discoloring. Arrange these over the tomatoes. Arrange the pepper rings on top and sprinkle with the spring onions. Tuck bunches of purslane or watercress round the plate and in between the tomato. Dot with pieces of crumbled crackers and capers and sprinkle with the remaining vinaigrette.

Ingredients
3 ripe tomatoes
2 green peppers, deseeded
3 tbsp olive oil
2 tbsp vinegar
pinch of salt
freshly ground black pepper
1 ripe pear
1 apple
2 spring onions, chopped
small bunch watercress
2 crackers
3 tbsp capers

Serves 4 as a tapa

Coca enramada
Pizza with garden vegetables

*C*ocas are quicker to make than to make the Italian pizza and contain no cheese. They are at root a peasant dish – but the combination of bread, vegetables and olive oil is delicious when the coca is enjoyed straight from the oven.

First make the pizza dough. Warm the milk to blood heat. Sift the flour into a food processor or big bowl and scatter with the salt. Add the dried yeast and 2 tablespoons of the oil to the bowl and work in enough of the warm milk to make a dough. If using a food processor, beat for 3–4 minutes, stopping every minute to break the dough up. Or turn the dough out onto a floured surface and knead it, pushing it out with the heel of one hand to a tongue shape, then folding and slapping it into a mound again. Do this until it becomes elastic. Shape the dough into a ball, put into an oiled bowl, cover with a cloth and leave in a warm place for 30 minutes, or a refrigerator for several hours. Preheat the oven to 220°C (425°F). Meanwhile sauté the onion in 3 tablespoons of oil.

When the dough has doubled in size, put it in the middle of an oiled 30-cm (12-inch) pizza plate or baking sheet. Press it down with your knuckles to fit the plate with a slight rim round the outside. Oil the edges of the dough and spread the onion over the dough. Distribute the peppers and tomato over the top and season with salt and pepper. Drizzle another tablespoon of oil over the top. Bake for 25–30 minutes.

Ingredients
150–175 ml (5–6 fl. oz) milk
250 g (9 oz) strong plain flour, plus extra for
  kneading
1 tsp salt
1½ tsp dried yeast
6 tbsp olive oil, plus extra
1 onion, finely chopped
2 small green peppers, deseeded and chopped
1 large ripe tomato, skinned and deseeded
salt and freshly ground black pepper

Serves 6 as a tapa

Flaò
Sweet cheesecake with mint

Ingredients

175 g (6 oz) plain flour, plus extra for rolling
pinch of salt
50 g (2 oz) chilled butter, diced, plus extra for
  greasing
5 small eggs
1 tbsp aniseed liqueur
1 tbsp milk
3 tbsp honey
5 oz superfine sugar
400 g (14 oz) full-fat cream cheese
15 fresh mint leaves
icing sugar, for dusting

Serves 8

*T*his is a very old recipe that appeared in the first cookbook printed in Spain, at the end of the fifteenth century. The cake is still made in Ibiza, especially at Easter time.

First make the pastry. Sift the flour and salt into a food processor or bowl. Cut in the fat, then beat in 1 egg and the aniseed liqueur, adding enough milk to help form a dough. Pull the pastry together into a ball and chill for 15 minutes.

Preheat the oven to 170°C (325°F). Place a heavy baking sheet in it to warm. Make the filling by beating the remaining eggs, sugar and honey together. Work in the cream cheese and mint leaves.

Roll out the pastry on a floured surface. Roll it round a rolling pin and lift this over a greased cake tin 25 cm (10 inches) in diameter, then press it into the tin. Pour in the filling, smooth the top and bake on the baking sheet for 40–50 minutes, until slightly risen and golden on top.

Leave it to cool for 5 minutes, then remove from the pan. Chill well. Dust with icing sugar before serving.

Ensaimadas
Majorcan sweet bread

A Majorcan favourite, ensaimadas are warm, yeast-based cakes fashioned into round, coiled shapes. Although delicious, these cakes are time-consuming to prepare, because the dough must be allowed to rise several times. Nevertheless, when time is available, these make delightful breakfast rolls. This recipe yields one very large, beautiful coil that can be sliced into individual portions. Serve with hot chocolate or steaming coffee.

Dissolve the yeast in the warmed milk and set aside.

Combine the sugar and salt together in a large bowl. Gradually add the flour and warm milk mixture. Blend thoroughly. Add the eggs and olive oil, mix well and knead until soft and well-blended. Cover with a damp cloth and leave to rise in a warm place for about 1 hour, or until the dough has doubled in volume.

Knead the dough again and using a rolling pin, roll the dough as thin as possible over a floured surface. Brush the entire surface of the dough with softened butter.

Start rolling the dough, bit by bit, from one side to the other (as if you were rolling up a poster). When the dough has been rolled up, allow it to rest for 1 hour.

After the dough has risen, coil it loosely, so that it resembles a snail shell. Transfer the coil to a greased baking sheet. Cover with an extremely large inverted bowl or bucket, large enough to ensure that the dough will not stick to the bowl's surface when it rises. Allow the dough to rise for several hours.

Preheat the oven to 190°C (375°F). Bake the dough coil for 45 minutes, or until the top is golden-brown. Brush the surface with melted butter and dust generously with sugar. To serve, cut into slices.

Ingredients
4 tsp dried yeast
225 ml (8 fl. oz) milk, warmed
100 g (4 oz) sugar, plus extra for dusting
1 tsp salt
450 g (1 lb) plain flour, plus extra for coating
2 large eggs
2 tbsp olive oil
6 oz butter, softened
butter, for brushing

Serves 8

Granizado
Iced lemonade sorbet

Ingredients
5 juicy lemons
600 ml (1 pint) boiling water
175 g (6 oz) sugar
600 ml (1 pint) cold water
crushed ice, to serve

Serves 10

S itting out under the trees at night, waiting for the first breath of cool air after a long, hot day, nothing is as refreshing as a lemon or coffee granizado.

Wash the lemons and pare the zest from them with a potato peeler. Halve them, squeeze out the juice and reserve it. Put the zest in a bowl and pour the boiling water over it. Leave until cold.

Remove the zest and stir in the sugar and lemon juice. Let stand for 5 minutes, then stir again, checking that the sugar has dissolved. Bottle and chill this lemonade.

To serve, pour the lemonade into a jug and add an equal amount of cold water. Fill tall glasses with crushed ice, pour the liquid over it and drink through straws.

CHAPTER 6

Central and Western Spain

This vast part of Spain takes in the capital Madrid as well as the regions of Castilla y Leon, Extremadura and La Mancha. The people of Castile were responsible for the creation of Spain as a country, spreading their culture and language across the Iberian peninsula. Today this part of the country remains culturally as well as geographically central. The characteristic features of its landscape include sunflowers, olive groves and windmills. This is where *Don Quixote* – the cornerstone of Spanish literature – was written; where the finest cheese, manchego, is produced; and where the production of saffron and fine wines is based.

A group of windmills in Campo de Criptana, a small town in La Mancha.

175

Sopa de lentejas, garbanzos y chorizo

Lentil, chick pea and chorizo soup

*C*horizo is popular throughout Spain and beyond, with its combination of fiery colour and spicy flavour making it the best-known Spanish sausage. The finest chorizo is made on the central plateaux, where the cool, dry air helps in the curing process.

Put the lentils in a large saucepan, pour in enough boiling water to cover them generously and simmer for about 20 minutes, until just tender. Drain well.

Heat the oil in the rinsed-out saucepan and gently fry the chorizo, onion and garlic for 4 minutes. Stir in the cumin, coriander, cinnamon and chilli, followed by the tomatoes, chick peas, tomato paste and stock. Bring to a boil, reduce the heat, cover and simmer for 15 minutes. Add salt and pepper and lemon juice to taste. Ladle the soup into bowls and serve.

Ingredients

100 g (4 oz) brown or green lentils
2 tbsp olive oil
50 g (2 oz) chorizo, chopped
1 onion, finely chopped
2 garlic cloves, crushed
3 tsp ground cumin
2 tsp ground coriander
½ tsp ground cinnamon
¼ tsp crushed dried chilli pepper
4 tomatoes, peeled, deseeded and chopped
400-g (14-oz) tin chick peas, rinsed and
  drained
1 tbsp tomato paste
1 litre (2 pints) vegetable or chicken stock
salt and freshly ground black pepper
juice of ½ lemon, to taste

Serves 4

Ensalada San Isidro
Saint Isidore mixed salad from Madrid

T *his salad traditionally opens the meal eaten during the festival of Saint Isidore the Labourer, patron saint of Madrid. The joyous celebrations occur in the middle of May, marking the death of the saint who has been associated with peasants and farmers for over a thousand years.*

First make the vinaigrette. Mash the garlic on a board with a pinch of salt, working with the flat of a knife or in a mortar. In a bowl or the mortar, stir in the vinegar, paprika and pepper, followed by the olive oil.

Soak the onion rings in water for 10 minutes, then drain and blot dry with paper towel. This helps remove the acrid aftertaste of strong onions.

Line the base of a shallow salad bowl or platter with lettuce. Flake the tuna over it, then decorate with the onion rings, sliced cooked eggs, cucumber and olives. Add the slices of tomato and the tinned asparagus, if using.

Sprinkle with some of the vinaigrette.

Ingredients

1 garlic clove, finely chopped
¼ tsp salt
3 tbsp sherry vinegar
pinch of paprika
freshly ground black pepper
90 ml (3½ fl. oz) olive oil
1 lettuce, washed and dried
200-g (7-oz) tin tuna, drained
1 onion, peeled and sliced into rings
2 hard-boiled eggs, peeled and sliced
½ cucumber, cut into chunks
6 tbsp small olives
2 tomatoes, sliced
250-g (9-oz) tin white asparagus, drained
  (optional)

Serves 4–6 as a tapa

Manchego al ajo y estragón
Manchego with garlic marinade and tarragon

*M*anchego is the glory of Spanish cheesemaking – milky and mild, with a slightly salty flavour and a very firm texture. Don't remove the rind before marinating.

Cut the cheese into small chunks and put in a jar or porcelain pot. Stir the vinegar into the olive oil and pour over the cheese. Chop the tarragon leaves finely. Crush the garlic clove and a few peppercorns. Sprinkle tarragon, garlic and pepper over the cheese. Mix everything well with clean hands.

Seal the jar or pot and leave for 4 days before eating.

Ingredients
450 g (1 lb) manchego cheese
2 tsp white wine vinegar
¼ pint olive oil
15-g (½-oz) bunch tarragon
1 clove garlic
black peppercorns

Serves 4–6 as a tapa

Pisto manchego
Stewed vegetables

Ingredients

2 large onions, thinly sliced

50 g (2 oz) raw ham or bacon, cubed
   (optional)

3 tbsp olive oil

3 garlic cloves, finely chopped

3 green peppers, deseeded and chopped

5 large ripe tomatoes, skinned and deseeded

3 courgettes, sliced

salt and freshly ground black pepper

pinch of ground nutmeg

4 tbsp chopped fresh parsley

4–8 eggs

Serves 4–8 as a tapa

Although best eaten hot with poached eggs, this mixture is also excellent served cold, with the eggs scrambled in and a little olive oil poured over. It is always worth making double the amount of pisto, if you have time, because it makes a very good sauce for meat. It will keep in an airtight container for 2–3 days in the fridge.

Fry the onions (and ham or bacon, if using) gently in the oil, adding the garlic towards the end. Add the peppers and fry for 5 minutes. Add the tomatoes and courgettes and cook over low heat, stirring occasionally, until the tomatoes reduce. Season well, adding the nutmeg and parsley.

The eggs may be broken into nests made in the mixture and lightly poached, or they may be scrambled in; or poach them separately and serve alongside the vegetables. The pisto may also be baked in a dish with the eggs in nests, which takes about 10 minutes in a medium oven (190°C/375°F).

Paella de verduras con pesto de nueces

Vegetable paella with walnut pesto

The combination of earthy walnut pesto with delicate, saffron-infused rice is simply magical. Chopped walnuts can be sprinkled on top of the paella to further enhance the nutty flavour of the rice.

First, make the walnut pesto. Place the basil leaves, chopped walnuts, grated cheese and garlic in a food processor and blend until a paste forms. With the motor still running, add the olive oil and walnut oil little by little, until well incorporated. Set the pesto aside.

Combine the chicken stock, white wine and saffron in a saucepan over low heat. Keep heated until ready for use.

To make the paella, heat the olive oil in a paella pan and sauté the onion and pepper over medium heat for several minutes. Mix in the mushrooms, courgettes, tomatoes, artichokes, parsley and paprika and cook for several minutes longer.

Pour in the rice and combine well. Stir in the stock mixture and pesto sauce and continue to cook until the liquid has been absorbed and the rice is tender. Serve warm and, if desired, sprinkled with chopped walnuts.

Ingredients

2 oz fresh basil leaves, finely chopped

3 tbsp chopped walnuts, plus extra to garnish (optional)

3 tbsp grated Manchego or Parmesan cheese

4 cloves garlic, finely chopped

4 tbsp olive oil

2 tbsp walnut oil

600 ml (1 pint) chicken stock

175 ml (6 fl. oz) dry white wine

½ tsp saffron

4 tbsp olive oil

1 small onion, finely chopped

1 medium red pepper, finely chopped

100 g (4 oz) oyster mushrooms, destemmed and chopped

100 g (4 oz) shiitake mushrooms, destemmed and chopped

2 courgettes, chopped

2 tomatoes, finely chopped

8 artichoke hearts, quartered

2 tbsp chopped parsley

½ tsp sweet paprika

325 g (12 oz) paella rice

Serves 6 as a main course, 8–10 as a tapa

Paella Extremeña
Extremaduran paella

Ingredients

175 ml (6 fl. oz) olive oil
225 g (8 oz) pork loin, cleaned and diced
225 g (8 oz) skinless, boneless chicken breasts, diced
2 medium onions, chopped
5 cloves garlic, finely chopped
225 g (8 oz) chorizo, case removed and crumbled or sliced
2 green peppers, cut into thin strips
2 large tomatoes, skinned, deseeded and chopped
450 g (1 lb) rice
1 litre (2 pints) beef stock
1 tsp turmeric
¼ tsp saffron
¼ tsp dried oregano
pinch of dried thyme
salt and freshly ground pepper, to taste
225 g (8 oz) Serrano ham, chopped

Serves 6 as a main course, 8–10 as a tapa

*A*lthough critics have dismissed the cuisine of Spain's arid Extremadura region as mere 'country cooking', it is slowly gaining popularity among those who appreciate basic, unadorned fare. Relying primarily on pork, ham, lamb and potatoes, recipes from Extremadura tend to be simple, yet immensely satisfying. This very filling paella, influenced by Extremaduran cuisine, features generous portions of Serrano ham, pork loin, chicken and chorizo (the delectable Spanish sausage which, some speculate, originated in Extremadura).

Heat half of the olive oil in a paella pan over medium heat. Add the pork and cook until done, about 10 minutes. Transfer to a different pan and set aside.

Cook the chicken in the paella pan until done, about 10 minutes. Transfer the chicken to the pan containing the pork.

Pour the remaining oil in the paella pan and sauté the onions for 5 minutes. Add the garlic and cook for a further 3 minutes. Add the chorizo sausage and cook for 5 minutes. Stir in the peppers and tomatoes and cook for a further 10 minutes over low heat.

Increase the heat to medium, add the rice to the pan and sauté for 5 minutes. Pour in the stock. Mix in the cooked pork and chicken and add the turmeric, saffron, oregano, thyme, salt and pepper. Cook for 15 minutes. Add the ham and cook for a further 7 minutes or until the liquid has been absorbed and the rice is tender.

Albóndigas al azafrán
Meatballs with saffron

Spaniards love meatballs and eat them often. In La Mancha it seems that saffron goes into every dish, too. The meatballs can be served plain, or with a simple sauce made by chopping, reducing and seasoning tomatoes.

Crumble the bread by hand or in a food processor and process or chop the ham or bacon. Mix in all the meat, lemon zest and juice, thyme, salt and cayenne pepper. Beat the eggs in a cup and stir in the saffron. Pour the eggs into the meatball mixture and combine. Put spoonfuls of this mixture on a floured baking sheet and roll to coat them with flour.

Fry the meatballs in hot oil, shaking the pan now and then so the meatballs roll over and take on a golden colour on all sides. Remove from the heat when the meatballs are cooked through. They take about 10 minutes.

Ingredients

2 slices stale bread
100 g (4 oz) ham or bacon
450 g (1 lb) minced pork or veal
pinch of finely grated lemon zest
1 tbsp lemon juice
pinch of dried thyme
½ tsp salt
pinch of cayenne pepper
2 large eggs
pinch of powdered saffron
6 tbsp flour
6 tbsp olive oil

Serves 4 as a main course, 6–8 as a tapa

Conejo al azafrán
Rabbit with saffron

Ingredients

2 large onions, chopped

7 tbsp olive oil

1 garlic clove, finely chopped

30 saffron strands

1 kg (2¼ lb) rabbit, in pieces

salt and freshly ground black pepper

250 ml (9 fl. oz) white wine

15 black peppercorns, lightly crushed

¼ tsp ground cumin

1 tsp paprika

pinch of cayenne pepper

6 sprigs fresh thyme

1 bay leaf

Serves 4 as a main course

*T*his is a rabbit dish rich with the tastes of La Mancha – highly spiced with thyme and also with cumin, which was introduced by the Arabs a millennium ago when they came to plant saffron.

Fry the onions slowly in 2 tablespoons of oil in a frying pan, adding the garlic as they soften. Powder the saffron strands with your fingers and soak in 4 tablespoons of hot water.

Remove the onion and garlic from the pan and add about 4 tablespoons more oil. Season the rabbit and fry the meaty portions (back legs and saddle) for 10 minutes. Tuck in the thinner pieces and fry for about another 10 minutes until everything is golden. Remove the rabbit and drain off all the oil.

Add the wine and stir to deglaze the pan. Pack the rabbit pieces tightly into an ovenproof dish and add the onion, wine, saffron liquid, crushed peppercorns, cumin, paprika and cayenne. Tuck in the thyme and the crumbled bay leaf. Add 100 ml (4 fl. oz) water to almost cover the meat. Cover and simmer very gently for about 1 hour until tender, making sure it does not get dry. Taste and add more seasonings. Be as bold as you dare – you're unlikely to season it more than the locals do!

Perdices a la Toledana
Partridges in wine with new potatoes

*S*hooting *partridges is a common sport in the hills behind Toledo, where this dish comes from and they are trapped all over the country as they fly through on their twice-yearly migration. The birds here are set off beautifully by the piquant wine sauce.*

Choose a heatproof dish into which the birds fit snugly. Season them inside and out with salt and pepper. Fry the birds in the oil, turning them over and propping them against the sides of the pan, until they are coloured on all sides. Remove and keep warm.

Fry the onion in the same oil, adding the garlic when it softens. Bed the birds down into the onion. Add the bay leaves, lemon zest, wine, vinegar and sufficient stock to cover the legs. Simmer, covered, over a low heat for about 15 minutes.

Meanwhile, in a separate saucepan, simmer the potatoes in boiling salted water for 10 minutes. Transfer to the dish, pushing them into the spaces between the birds. Continue cooking until the potatoes are done.

Remove the potatoes and the birds. Halve the partridges and arrange in a warm serving dish. Surround them with the potatoes. Keep warm. Discard the bay leaves and lemon zest and blend the remaining contents of the dish in a blender or food processor. Reheat and check the seasoning. Pour a little of the sauce over the birds and sprinkle with parsley. Pass the remaining sauce round in a jug.

Ingredients

3 fat partridges, wishbones removed
salt and freshly ground black pepper
3 tbsp olive oil
1 large onion, chopped
3 garlic cloves, finely chopped
3 bay leaves
1 strip lemon zest
175 ml (6 fl. oz) dry white wine
4 tbsp sherry vinegar
200 ml (7 fl. oz) chicken stock
24 baby new potatoes
chopped fresh parsley

Serves 6 as a main course

Cochifrito
Fried lamb with lemon juice

Ingredients

775 g (1¾ lb) tender lamb
salt and freshly ground black pepper
2 tbsp olive oil
1 onion, chopped
2 tsp paprika
2 garlic cloves, finely chopped
250 ml (9 fl. oz) lamb stock or water
juice of 1 lemon
2 tbsp chopped fresh parsley

Serves 6 as a main course

*C*astilian lamb is always superb. In restaurants the animal is baked whole in large, domed ovens. At home it is more likely to be fried simply, often with lemon juice.

Trim excess fat from the lamb and cut the meat into strips. Season with salt and pepper. Heat the oil in a large, heavy-based saucepan over your hottest burner. Add the meat and onion and turn constantly with a wooden spoon until the meat is sealed on all sides.

When the meat is golden and the onion is soft, sprinkle with paprika and add the garlic. Cook for a couple more minutes, then pour in the stock or water. Continue cooking over medium heat until the liquid has virtually gone.

Sprinkle with lemon juice and parsley, cover and simmer for 5 minutes. Check the seasonings before serving.

A shepherd near Cuenca driving his flock home along a country road.

Patatas a la importancía
Potatoes made special

This is an excellent potato dish to precede roast meat, but it also makes a modest supper dish if served with tinned salmon flaked over the top.

Turn the potato cubes in well-seasoned flour, then dip into the beaten eggs, flipping them to coat. Pour oil into a frying pan to come 1 cm (½ inch) deep and heat. Fry the potatoes in batches, turning them regularly. When browned, remove from the pan and transfer to paper towel to drain, while you cook the next batch.

Meanwhile fry the onion in 2 tablespoons of oil in a wide, shallow saucepan, adding the garlic as the onion softens. Add the potatoes, packing them in well. Pour in the wine, dissolve the saffron in the stock and add to the pan, together with the bay leaf and parsley. Season gently and simmer, covered, for 20 minutes.

Ingredients

4 large potatoes, diced
6 tbsp flour
salt and freshly ground black pepper
2 large eggs, beaten
oil, for frying
1 onion, finely chopped
2 garlic cloves, finely chopped
100 ml (4 fl. oz) dry white wine
pinch powdered saffron
250 ml (9 fl. oz) chicken stock
1 bay leaf
4 tbsp chopped fresh parsley

Serves 4–6 as an accompaniment

Spanish field workers harvesting potatoes.

Lentejas a la perfecta
Perfect lentils

Ingredients
225 g (½ lb) green lentils
salt
4 garlic cloves, finely chopped
1 thick slice country bread
4 tbsp olive oil
2 tbsp red wine vinegar

Serves 4 as an accompaniment

*I*n central Spain, lentils are often cooked with different parts of the pig – ears, sausages, belly and so on. Cooked plain, as here, they go well with fried sausages, chorizo, or roast pork.

Bring the lentils to a simmer in a large saucepan full of water, adding salt only when they are done, after about 30 minutes.

Meanwhile, fry the garlic and bread in olive oil in a frying pan. When the bread is golden on both sides, tip the contents of the frying pan – including the oil – into a mortar or blender and reduce to a paste. Add the vinegar and stir to combine.

Pour off the water in the saucepan, except for a couple of spoonfuls, and stir in the bread paste. Simmer for a minute to allow the flavours to blend.

CHAPTER 7

Andalusia

CÓRDOBA

SEVILLE

Andalusia

GRANADA

ALMERIA

JEREZ

MALAGA

GIBRALTAR

This southern region has been home to numerous successive cultures, most importantly the Moors, whose residence here for many centuries in the Middle Ages has left a clear stamp on the architecture, culture and gastronomy. The culinary centre of Andalusia is Seville, famous for its excellent grilled seafood, the local speciality ham, jamón ibérico, lamb's kidneys in a sherry sauce and the deliciously refreshing cold soup, gazpacho. Many of these and other Andalusian dishes, are legacies of the Moorish presence – think, for example, of the deep-fried pastries bathed in honey which are often served as a dessert.

The Alhambra was formerly the residence of the Moorish rulers of Andalusia. Today, its splendid Islamic architecture makes the palace one of the biggest tourist attractions in the country.

Gazpachuelo
Potato and fish soup

The vinegar in this warm soup is the link with gazpacho. It is surprisingly good and easy to make, so in Spain it is associated with emergencies! The idea is to stretch fish for one or two people to make soup for six.

Put the stock or water, potatoes and salt in a large saucepan. Cook until the potatoes are almost tender, then add the fish, cut into small pieces, and cook for a further 5 minutes. Transfer the potatoes and fish to a serving bowl.

Let the stock cool a little. Stir the mayonnaise into the stock to make a creamy soup. Pour the soup over the potatoes and fish. Check the seasoning, stir in the vinegar and serve warm. Sometimes a jug of vinegar is passed round at the table.

Ingredients

900 ml (1¼ pints) fish stock or water

700 g (1½ lb) new potatoes

½ tsp salt

1–2 small fish (such as red mullet or sole), scaled and filleted

300 ml (10 fl. oz) mayonnaise (homemade if possible)

2 tbsp white wine vinegar

Serves 6

Pimientos asados al ajo
Roasted peppers with garlic

Roasting the peppers for this recipe makes them taste deliciously smoky; they are then stewed slowly with a sweet–sour, intensely garlicky sauce, making a wonderful combination of flavours.

Place the peppers in a large, heavy saucepan with the sliced garlic and the olive oil. Sprinkle with salt and cover. Cook gently, covered, for about 20 minutes over very low heat, turning once or twice.

When the peppers are very tender, remove the lid and increase the heat to medium-high. Add the balsamic vinegar, then remove from the heat and add the white wine vinegar. Pour into a bowl and allow to cool. When cold, add more salt and wine vinegar if wished.

Ingredients
3 each: red and yellow peppers, roasted,
　peeled and cut into bite-size pieces
15–20 cloves garlic, thinly sliced
90 ml (3½ fl. oz) olive oil
salt to taste
balsamic vinegar to taste
white wine vinegar to taste

Serves 4–6 as a tapa

Pinchitos morunos
Spicy Moorish kebabs

*E*urope's first kebabs were brought by the Arabs from Africa. They are eaten everywhere in Spain as a tapa, though nowadays they are made from pork rather than the original lamb. Spices for them are sold ready-mixed in Andalusia. Curry powder has been used as part of this mixture, as it contains cumin and the identical herbs.

Crush the garlic with the salt in a mortar, then work in the other ingredients. Skewer the pork, 3 or 4 cubes on a small stick, place them in a small dish, and add the garlic and spice mixture, turning so they are well coated. Marinate for at least a couple of hours.

Spread the pinchitos out well on a barbecue or on foil under a hot grill. Cook them for about 3 minutes on each side.

Ingredients
2 garlic cloves, finely chopped
2 tsp salt
450 g (1 lb) lean pork, cubed
1 tsp mild curry powder
½ tsp coriander seeds
1 tsp paprika
¼ tsp dried thyme
freshly ground black pepper
3 tbsp olive oil
1 tbsp lemon juice

Serves 6 as a tapa

Gazpacho Andaluz
Classic Andalusian gazpacho

*T*his basic version of gazpacho is the one travellers would be most likely to encounter when touring through Spain. The fact that this soup is commonly found, however, in no way renders it 'ordinary'. One taste of this chilled gazpacho and you will be instantly transported to a land of whitewashed walls, red-tiled roofs and a golden sun.

Combine the olive oil, vinegar, garlic, salt, cumin and Tabasco sauce in a food processor with half of the vegetables, and reduce to a purée. Transfer the soup mixture to a large bowl. Purée the remaining vegetables and add to the soup. Add ice cubes (or water) to taste and additional salt if necessary. Refrigerate until very cool, or overnight.

Before serving, garnish the gazpacho with the chopped tomatoes, croûtons and diced hard-boiled eggs.

Ingredients

100 ml (4 fl. oz) olive oil
50 ml (2 fl. oz) red wine vinegar
3 cloves garlic, chopped
1 tbsp salt
¼ tsp ground cumin
⅛ tsp Tabasco sauce
4 large ripe tomatoes, sliced
900 g (2 lb) tinned plum tomatoes
1 green pepper, sliced
1 cucumber, sliced
½ onion, sliced
ice cubes
chopped tomatoes, to garnish
croûtons, to garnish
hard-boiled eggs, diced, to garnish

Serves 8

Gazpacho verde
Green gazpacho

*T*his colourful variation on the traditional red gazpacho hails from Huelva and the Sierra Morena in Andalusia. Unlike the classic gazpacho recipes, this soup relies on spinach, lettuce, parsley and mint for its freshness and texture. Although it is quite different from its more traditional gazpacho cousins, this version is every bit as refreshing.

In a blender, combine the lettuce, spinach, spring onions, chilli, cucumber and parsley until the mixture forms a purée. Gradually add in the chicken stock, sour cream, mayonnaise, mint, white pepper and salt. Purée the mixture until it reaches an even consistency. Refrigerate the soup until you are ready to serve.

Serve the soup chilled in individual bowls, with a spoonful of soured cream over each serving, if desired.

Ingredients

100 g (4 oz) lettuce leaves, chopped
100 g (4 oz) spinach
3 spring onions, diced
½ red chilli pepper, deseeded and chopped
½ cucumber, peeled and diced
1 tbsp chopped parsley
475 ml (16 fl. oz) chicken stock
100 ml (4 fl. oz) sour cream, plus extra to garnish (optional)
100 ml (4 fl. oz) mayonnaise
1 tsp chopped fresh mint leaves
½ tsp white pepper
½ tsp salt

Serves 4–6

Gazpacho blanco
White gazpacho

This dish is a modern adaptation of Malaga's ajo blanco. Unlike ajo blanco, however, this version omits the almonds and relies on soured cream and yogurt for its unmistakable creamy texture.

Working in two batches, purée all the ingredients except for the almonds and grapes in a food processor. Combine both batches in a large bowl and refrigerate for several hours or overnight.

Immediately before serving, garnish individual servings with the diced bell pepper and tomatoes and the croûtons.

Ingredients
3 medium cucumbers, peeled and chopped
3 cloves garlic, chopped
475 ml (16 fl. oz) soured cream
225 ml (8 fl. oz) plain yogurt
225 ml (8 fl. oz) chicken stock
salt and pepper, to taste
⅛ teaspoon Tabasco sauce
½ green pepper, deseeded and diced
2 small tomatoes, deseeded and diced
croûtons

Serves 6

Ajo blanco
Chilled white almond soup

Ingredients
175 g (6 oz) blanched almonds
4 slices crustless white bread, soaked in cold
   water for 5 minutes
3 garlic cloves, sliced
5 tbsp olive oil
600 ml (1 pint) cold water
2 tbsp sherry vinegar
salt
75 g (3 oz) seedless green grapes
toasted slivered almonds (optional)
chopped fresh parsley (optional)

Serves 4–6

A jo blanco, a white version of gazpacho, is believed to have originated with the Moors. If a silkier texture is desired, try soaking the blanched almonds in milk before processing. This will enhance the soup's delicate creaminess.

Combine the almonds, bread and garlic in a food processor and blend until smooth. With the motor still running, slowly pour in the olive oil until a smooth paste is formed. Add in the cold water and the vinegar. Process until the mixture is thin and smooth. Season with salt to taste.

Pour the mixture into a large bowl. Float the grapes on the top of the soup. Cover and allow to chill in the refrigerator. To serve, pour the soup into individual soup bowls and garnish with the toasted almond slivers and chopped parsley, if desired.

Higaditos de pollo con vinagre de Jerez
Chicken livers with sherry vinegar

*T*he term 'sherry' is an anglicization of Jerez – the name of the Andalusian city which is the centre of sherry production. The Moors, in the eighth century, introduced the fortification of wine to southern Spain and sherry was the most notable result. Here it is used to transform chicken livers into a fine, rich dish.

Wash and trim the chicken livers to remove the green bile sacs and any gristle.

Mix the paprika, garlic, salt and pepper together in a bowl. Toss the livers in the mixture, to coat.

Melt half the butter in a large saucepan. Add the livers and cook over high heat, stirring continuously, until sealed and browned all over. Place livers in a warmed bowl.

Add the onion to the pan and soften over a lower heat. Increase the heat again, add the vinegar and sugar and cook until the vinegar is greatly reduced. Add the stock, stir and reduce to half the quantity.

Cut the remaining butter into small pieces, add to the pan and stir until it melts into the liquid. Check the seasoning and pour the sauce over the livers. Serve in a large bowl or in smaller, individual ones.

Ingredients
450 g (1 lb) chicken livers
1 tsp paprika
1 tsp garlic
½ tsp each salt and freshly
    ground black pepper
100 g (4 oz) butter, melted
½ onion, finely chopped
50 ml (2 fl. oz) sherry vinegar
1 tsp sugar
300 ml (½ pint) chicken stock

Serves 4 as a main course, 6 as a tapa

Sherry barrels in a cellar in Jerez.

Riñones en salsa de Jerez
Kidneys in sherry sauce

Ingredients

700 g (1½ lb) lamb or veal kidneys
175 ml (6 fl. oz) olive oil
2 tsp garlic, crushed
1 tsp paprika
2 onions, chopped
90 ml (3½ fl. oz) sherry
300 ml (½ pint) chicken stock
salt and freshly ground
   black pepper
fresh thyme sprigs

Serves 6 as a tapa

Lamb and veal kidneys are tender and flavourful. Avoid overcooking them, as this can make them unpleasantly tough.

Clean the kidneys, removing the hard core and any fat. Slice thinly with a sharp knife.

Bring a saucepan of water to a boil and plunge the kidneys in for one minute to remove the bitterness.

Heat the oil and fry half the kidneys with 1 teaspoon of the garlic and ½ teaspoon of the paprika. Cook quickly, stirring so that the garlic does not burn. When cooked, blend to a purée in a food processor. Set aside.

In the same pan, cook the onions until soft. Place the remaining kidneys in the pan with the other teaspoon of garlic, the remaining paprika, the sherry and the stock. Bring to the boil.

Lower the heat, add the puréed kidneys, stir and simmer until the whole kidneys are tender (approximately 5 minutes). Season and serve garnished with sprigs of thyme.

Paella de picadillo
Paella with picadillo

*T*his Andalusian-inspired paella incorporates picadillo, a light dish served throughout southern Spain during the summer. Traditionally a mixture of oil, peppers, onions, garlic, tomato and meat (typically chicken or beef), picadillo is widely popular throughout Andalusia and takes only minutes to prepare. Here, picadillo is deliciously paired with paella, creating a more filling main-course meal. This works well as a refreshing lunch or an informal dinner.

Add the raisins to the warmed sherry and set aside. In a large, heavy-bottomed saucepan, cook the sausage, minced beef, chorizo, onion and garlic over medium heat until the meat is cooked and browned. Drain off the fat. Stir in the raisins and sherry, the undrained tomatoes, the chillies, sugar, cinnamon, cumin and cloves. Bring to a boil, reduce the heat and cook, uncovered, for 30 minutes or until almost all the liquid has evaporated, stirring occasionally.

Heat the olive oil in a paella pan. Add the rice and sauté for 5 minutes. Pour in the stock and saffron and cook for 20 minutes. Add the sausage mixture, stir and cook for a further 5 minutes or until the rice is tender and the liquid has been absorbed. Serve immediately.

Ingredients

65 g (2½ oz) raisins
50 ml (2 fl. oz) dry sherry, warmed
225 g (8 oz) pork sausage
225 g (8 oz) lean minced beef
100 g (4 oz) chorizo sausage
1 onion, peeled and chopped
3 cloves garlic, minced
400-g (14-oz) tin diced tomatoes
100 g (4 oz) mild green bottled chillies, drained and diced
2 tbsp sugar
1 tsp ground cinnamon
¼ tsp ground cumin
⅛ tsp ground cloves
2 tbsp olive oil
325 g (12 oz) paella rice
900 ml (1½ pints) beef stock
¼ tsp saffron

Serves 6 as a main course, 8–10 as a tapa

Pato a la Sevillana
Duck with oranges and olive, Seville style

Ingredients

1 oven-ready duck
salt and freshly ground black pepper
2 tbsp olive oil
1 onion, finely chopped
1 green pepper, deseeded and chopped
1 large tomato, skinned, deseeded and
   chopped
1 tbsp flour
200 ml (7 fl. oz) fino sherry
1 Seville orange (or 1 sweet orange plus
   ½ lemon)
1 bay leaf
8–10 parsley stalks, bruised
150–300 ml (5–10 fl. oz) duck or chicken stock
2 large carrots
150 g (5 oz) green olives

Serves 4 as a main course

*T*he original 'duck with orange' comes from the city that introduced bitter oranges to Europe in the eleventh century. Their sharp juice and the salty olives make the duck seem fatless. Since it is a party dish, an elegant modern presentation is given here.

Quarter the duck, removing the backbone, visible fat and hanging skin. Season and prick the remaining skin well. Heat the oil in a large, heavy-bottomed saucepan and brown the duck on all sides.

Remove the duck and all but 2 tablespoons of fat from the saucepan. Fry the onion in the pan until soft, adding the pepper and tomato halfway through. Sprinkle with flour and stir in. Add the sherry and stir until simmering.

Fit the duck pieces back into the saucepan compactly, tucking in the backbone and 2 strips of thinly pared orange zest. Slice the orange (and lemon, if using) without peeling it and tuck the slices round the duck, pushing in the bay leaf and parsley stalks. Add enough stock to almost cover and simmer with the lid on for 45 minutes.

Quarter the carrots lengthwise, remove the cores and cut them into olive-sized lengths. In a separate saucepan, simmer them in boiling water for 5 minutes.

Remove the duck pieces and discard the backbone, parsley stalks, orange zest and bay leaf. Purée the sauce through a vegetable mill or blender. Reurn the duck to the saucepan and pour in the sauce. Add the olives and carrot pieces and simmer for another 10 minutes or until the carrots are tender.

Move the duck pieces to a serving dish with a slotted spoon. Surround with the carrots and olives and keep warm. If there is too much sauce, boil to reduce it a little. Any floating fat can be removed by laying strips of paper towel across the surface, then lifting them off. Check the seasoning, pour the sauce over the duck and serve.

Habas a la rondeña
Broad beans with ham, Ronda style

*I*n Spain this dish is made with raw Serrano ham, which is why it is known as 'Ronda style' even though it is eaten everywhere – the sierras of Ronda are famous for their hams from the black-footed pig. In summer, when parsley is difficult to find in the south, the garnish may be diced red pepper or tomato.

Fry the onion in the oil in a large, heavy-bottomed saucepan. As it starts to soften, add the ham and garlic and fry until lightly browned. Stir in the beans (frozen beans need no water; fresh ones need 100 ml/4 fl. oz). Cover and simmer until tender, stirring occasionally. Fresh or frozen, they take about 10 minutes.

Season the beans generously, stir in the chopped eggs and heat through. Stir in the parsley and serve.

Ingredients
175 g (6 oz) onion, chopped
4 tbsp olive oil
175 g (6 oz) raw ham
1 garlic clove, finely chopped
900 g (2 lb) young podded (or frozen) broad beans
salt and freshly ground black pepper
4 hard-boiled eggs, peeled and chopped
50 g (2 oz) fresh parsley, chopped

Serves 6 as a tapa

Helado de pasas de Málaga
Málaga raisin ice cream

Ingredients

100 g (4 oz) muscatel raisins
vanilla ice cream to serve 4
250 ml (9 fl. oz) Málaga wine or sweet
   oloroso sherry

Serves 4

*I*ce cream is very popular in the south of Spain, but rarely made at home. This rich, sweet dessert is based on shop-bought vanilla ice cream – but few mass-produced varieties have the kind of elegant flavour which you can obtain by adding raisins and sweet wine.

Pour about 4 tablespoons of boiling water over the raisins and leave to soak for 2 hours. Drain and fold them into the vanilla ice cream, then spoon into 4 bowls. Pour the wine or sherry over and serve.

Index

Picture credits

The images in this book are used with the permission of the copyright holders stated below. (Images are listed by page number.) All other illustrations and pictures are © Quintet Publishing Limited. While every effort had been made to credit contributors, Quintet Publishing would like to apologise should there have been any omissions or errors, and would be pleased to make the appropriate correction for future editions of this book.

2 Shutterstock; 3 Shutterstock; 6 Spanish Tourist Office; 7 Shutterstock; 8 Shutterstock; 10 Shutterstock; 11 Shutterstock; 12 Shutterstock; 13 Shutterstock; 14 Jon Arnold Images Ltd / Alamy; 15 Spanish Tourist Office; 16 Shutterstock; 17 Shutterstock; 18 Shutterstock; 19 Shutterstock; 20 Shutterstock; 21 Spanish Tourist Office; 22 Shutterstock; 23 Shutterstock; 24 Spanish Tourist Office; 25 Shutterstock; 26 Shutterstock; 33 Shutterstock; 39 Stephen Conroy Photography Ltd. / Stockfood America; 40 Amiand, Francis / Stockfood America; 44 Thelma & Louise / Stockfood America; 52 Shutterstock; 55 Shooter, Howard / Stockfood America; 56 carmen sedano / Alamy; 59 Loftus, D. / Stockfood America; 63 Shutterstock; 64 Morgans, Gareth / Stockfood America; 68 Shutterstock; 72 Bichon, Franck / Stockfood America; 74 Foodfolio / Stockfood America; 75 Poplis, Paul / Stockfood America; 76 Shutterstock; 79 Shutterstock; 80 Cazals, Jean / Stockfood America; 83 FoodPhotogr. Eising / Stockfood America; 84 Schliack, Amos / Stockfood America; 85 Shutterstock; 89 Roger Day / Alamy; 90 Stempell, Ruprecht / Stockfood America; 93 McConnell & McNamara / Stockfood America; 94 Gastromedia / Alamy; 97 Teubner Foodfoto / Stockfood America; 98 Shutterstock; 100 Shutterstock; 101 FoodPhotogr. Eising / Stockfood America; 103 DeLuca, Sara / Stockfood America; 104 Urban, Martina / Stockfood America; 107 Studio Bonisolli / Stockfood America; 112 Shutterstock; 115 Shutterstock; 119 Buchanan, Steve / Stockfood America; 122 Shutterstock; 124 Spanish Tourist Office; 128 JUPITERIMAGES/ Agence Images / Alamy; 135 FoodPhotogr. Eising / Stockfood America; 136 Gastromedia / Alamy; 139 Shutterstock; 140 Shutterstock; 144 Shutterstock; 147 Arras, Klaus / Stockfood America; 148 Bischof, Harry / Stockfood America; 151 Strauß, F. / Stockfood America; 152 Shutterstock; 159 Holsten, Ulrike / Stockfood America; 164 Shutterstock; 166 Shutterstock; 167 Shutterstock; 168 Rynio / Stockfood America; 171 Feiler Fotodesign / Stockfood America; 172 Marcialis, Renato / Stockfood America; 174 Spanish Tourist Board; 178 Buntrock, Gerrit Ltd. / Stockfood America; 179 Carriere, James / Stockfood America; 180 Maria Galan Still / Alamy; 187 Schliack, Amos / Stockfood America; 188 Arras, Klaus / Stockfood America; 191 Cazals, Jean / Stockfood America; 192 G P Bowater / Alamy; 195 Balzerek, Reinhard / Stockfood America; 196 Heinze, Winfried / Stockfood America; 198 Shutterstock; 201 Shutterstock; 202 Shutterstock; 203 Shutterstock; 205 Carlén, Hans / Stockfood America; 206 Shutterstock; 207 FoodPhotogr. Eising / Stockfood America; 208 Grilly, Bernard / Stockfood America; 211 Shutterstock; 212 Kirchherr / Stockfood America; 216 Newedel, Karl / Stockfood America; 219 Rivière, Jean-Francois / Stockfood America; 220 Marcialis, Renato / Stockfood America